American Indian Lives

WOODY KIPP

Viet Cong at Wounded Knee

The Trail of a Blackfeet Activist

University of Nebraska Press, Lincoln and London

Library of Congress
Cataloging-in-Publication
Data
Kipp, Woody.
Viet Cong at Wounded Knee :
the trail of a Blackfeet activist /
Woody Kipp.
p. cm.— (American Indian lives)
ISBN 0-8032-2760-4 (cloth: alk.
paper)—ISBN 0-8032-0426-4
(electronic)
ISBN 978-0-8032-1641-9 (paper:
alk. paper)
1. Kipp, Woody.   2. Piegan
Indians—Biography.   3. Piegan
Indians—Social conditions.
4. Piegan Indians—Civil rights.
5. Indian veterans—Montana—
Cut Bank—Biography.
6. Wounded Knee (S.D.)—
History—Indian occupation,
1973.   I. Title.   II. Series.
E99.P58K57 2004
978.6004'97352–dc22
2004001480
Set in Galliard
by Kim Essman.
Designed by Dika Eckersley

Contents

VIET CONG AT WOUNDED KNEE

Branding

1

I, Woody Kipp, Natoos Sina (Sun Chief), survived on bull elk meat for a few days when I was two months old. In mid-December 1945 the snow piled deep, the drifts towered, and then came the wind. The deep snows of northern Montana are legendary, and the wind can roar off the east slope of the Continental Divide at more than a hundred miles per hour. High in the reaches of Glacier National Park is an alpine lake from which the bull elk comes forth, shaking his horns and creating the swift-moving storms that rake the Blackfeet homeland. The Pikuni Blackfeet – we still have some who speak the mother tongue – know the elk as *ponokah stumiks*. The Elk Nation is represented in the medicine bundles of the Blackfeet.

Just above the Blackfeet agency town of Browning, Montana, the wind sometimes lifts empty railroad flatcars off the track and hurls them down the embankment. Constant wind is a way of life for the Pikuni Blackfeet. The old-timers say the Great Mystery sings in the wind and they compose their songs by listening to it blow.

Wind, deep snow, and bitter cold. Blackfoot Country.

My adopted folks, Joe and Isabell Kipp, lived on Cut Bank Creek in the approximate heart of the Blackfeet Indian Reservation. They didn't have a car in 1945.

Although the name Kipp grows from Germanic roots, it has been a part of the Blackfoot Confederacy for a few generations.[1] Some Blackfeet are Kipps by blood, some by adoption, and some by marriage. Joe W. Kipp, my adopted father, was a full-blood Pikuni Blackfoot Indian. (The *W* in his name distinguishes him from another Joe Kipp, a well-known Indian trader who was alive when my adopted father was born). The Pikuni are one of three divisions of the ancient Blackfoot Confederacy. According to historians they were a fierce group, fighting with all the tribes in the northern plains region once they acquired the gun and the horse. The Blackfoot Confederacy controlled the northern plains from the Yellowstone River, which runs through the current Montana city of Billings, north into the Canadian provinces of Alberta and Saskatchewan. It was a pretty good-sized ranch we had, and there weren't any fences on it. Modern men can only guess at that kind of freedom. Like nearly all present-day reservations, the Pikuni Blackfeet Reservation is miniscule compared to the tribe's landholdings when the Europeans arrived.

James Kipp – father of the Indian trader Joe Kipp – apparently came out of Canada about 1830 in the employ of the fur trade. He married a Mandan woman, the granddaughter of Four Bears. Their son, Joe Kipp, became an Indian trader and married a Blackfoot woman. Joe Kipp, described as one of the "Merchant Princes of the Upper Missouri," traded with the three Blackfoot bands, the Pikuni, the Kainah (commonly known as the Bloods, located in Canada just across the border from the Blackfeet Reservation), and the Blackfoot proper, the Siksika (who live east of the Canadian city of Calgary). We speak a common language and have a common culture; we are leaves of the same sacred tree.

Because of their avowed ferocity toward other tribes and whites, the U.S. Army marked the Pikuni for slaughter in 1870. The slaughter, known as Baker's Massacre, took place on the Marias River on January 23, 1870, a short distance south of the present town of Shelby, Montana.[2] More than one version exists as to why and how the U.S. Army targeted the Pikuni band of Chief Heavy Runner for military action, an action that culminated in the death of more than 170 Pikuni, mainly women and children and elderly, while the able-bodied men were hunting buffalo near Sweet Grass Hills (a misnomer, since the true Blackfeet designation for the spot was Sweet Pine Hills) in the dead of winter. When the men returned they found their families had been killed and burned on funeral pyres by the army men.

Joe Kipp, by the time of the massacre, had traded with the Blackfoot tribes for years. He had acted as guide for the army in finding the Blackfoot camp that was slaughtered. Anguished over the massacre, which he did not participate in and did not condone, Joe Kipp adopted some of the children who had survived by hiding. One of those children was my adopted father's father, John Kipp (Night Gun), and that's how my full-blood adopted father came to have a Germanic surname. He was a Heavy Runner.

In the latter part of the nineteenth century John Kipp became widely known on the Blackfeet reservation as Cut Bank John Kipp, being the first of the Blackfeet to live permanently on Cut Bank Creek. After his adoption Cut Bank John lived and worked around the trading post, became quite wealthy, and built a large, fancy two-story house on Cut Bank Creek. I spent time in that house as a child.

His son, Joe Kipp, and Joe's wife Isabell lived the better part of their lives on a river bottom, which was the land allotted by the U.S. government on Cut Bank Creek. Joe Kipp, whose Indian name was Eagle Shoe, was a tall, dark, full-blood Blackfeet Indian. He used to break horses sixteen at a time in his younger years; scotch-hobbling them (tying a hind foot up to keep them somewhat quiet) and then getting on one after another until they were rideable. Eagle Shoe's brand was Triangle Bar Z (the brand is registered in my name today). Isabell was a half-blood; her father, George Cook, was a white man of whom I know nearly nothing. She and hundreds of others were schooled at the old Catholic Family Mission, built on land given to the Catholics by White Calf. Isabell was in fact my biological mother's aunt, so I was a blood part of the family into which I was adopted. I've been a Kipp since I was nine days old.

I am Blackfeet through my mother's blood. She was a Wolverine on her mother's side and a Munro on her father's side. Hugh Munro was one of the first white men to live permanently with the people of the Blackfoot Confederacy, coming among them in 1815 as a goodwill ambassador for the Hudson's Bay Company (beaver pelts lured the Hudson's Bay men out onto the western plains of North America). Hugh Munro could have lived quite a comfortable life had he chosen to return to Three Rivers near Montreal, but he chose instead to run buffalo over the plains at forty miles per hour. He remained with the Pikuni Blackfeet until his death in 1896 at the age of ninety-eight.

All I know of my biological father is his name. He left not long after I was born and never returned. His name was Roger Van Ness – that Dutch- or German-sounding name doesn't mean much to me. I was raised in the Pikuni Blackfeet world. I'm a powwow dancer, and it'd be awful hard to dance in wooden shoes.

When I was adopted in late 1945, Joe Kipp was fifty-seven years old, Isabell was fifty-two, and they had already raised a family. Three sons and two daughters had survived, and a couple of others died in infancy, which was fairly common in a time marked by whooping cough, diphtheria, and other diseases for which there were no vaccines. Though I never knew them, I heard my mom and pop talk of Norman and Elizabeth, who had died in infancy.

Their oldest daughter, Aurise, was my godmother and became a World War II veteran. She represented that generation of Blackfeet who had been thoroughly brainwashed by white society as children.[3] She found little to redeem about our Native culture. The schoolteachers on the reservation, the churches, and the people of the previous generation who had been brainwashed, all effectively encouraged her to emulate white women. She married a half-blood whose father owned and operated a gas station and grocery store on the reservation. With most of the reservation people living on welfare, being married to someone associated with local commerce was undoubtedly satisfying to her. She and her husband often worked on large ranches in Montana; he served as a ranch foreman, and she cooked for the ranch hands. Aurise died in March of 1998 after lying in the Veterans Hospital in Columbia Falls, Montana, for several years. Her mind remained clear nearly to the end.

Katherine was next in age after Aurise. She was psychic and her spirits were something we feared, something to make one deathly afraid of the dark. Katherine sadly lived an extremely hardscrabble life with a mixed-blood husband, John "Jack" Hirst, who was an alcoholic. She died in a head-on collision with tourists in the summer of 1973. The Hirst name would become very well known in the Cut Bank area after the mysterious and contentious death of their son, Clayton, in the Glacier County jail in March of 1975. A medicine man, in a ceremony, said he died at the hands of three white men who had entered his cell. It could not be proven in a white Montana court, however. *Rolling Stone* magazine considered doing a story on the death of Clayton Hirst but later declined to do so. One morning, about a year after Clayton's death, I saw a very bright spot in the azure sky to the northeast of where I was living in Heart Butte. I learned later during a spirit ceremony, which was presided over by Sam Spotted Eagle, that the bright spot had been my nephew's message that he was okay.

My oldest adopted brother was John Kipp – Big John. He *was* big, standing six foot three and weighing about 230 pounds. He always stayed in shape. When a man is that large and fit, he's dangerous. He trapped many beaver, one time catching twenty-six in a single night. He served in the marine infantry on Iwo Jima and Guam during World War II. Once, he was commended for carrying a Japanese soldier up a hill to a command center for interrogation during the battle for Iwo Jima. When my pop told this story to his friends outside of a grocery story in Browning, they wanted to know Big John's Indian name. He had never been named in the Indian way, but an old woman who was a friend of the family immediately called him Kiyotokan, Bear Head, after an uncle that Big John had followed around as a child. Names in the old way carried weight. Big John was recalled to active duty during the Korean War but did not have to leave the states; he spent his time at Camp Pendleton in California. Upon release from active duty, he returned to Cut Bank Creek.

While he held to many of the hunting and gathering ways he had been raised with, Big John was also a progressive who seemed to have no trouble using and adapting aspects of white society that he found useful. In the 1950s, the government sponsored a farm and ranch seminar for veterans. John was practically the only Indian on the reservation who took the farm training; some other Indians went the ranching route. My folks owned a few hundred acres of rangeland that had been allotted to them and their children. John used a loan through the tribal credit program to buy a secondhand tractor and plow. He broke the rangeland into farmland and started raising wheat and barley, successfully. In 1956 he bought a brand-new black Ford Fairlane, followed a year later by a new two-tone green International four-wheel drive flatbed 3/4-ton truck, one of the first four-wheel drive vehicles on the Blackfeet Reservation. Big John would be making close to a hundred thousand a year by the time he died. Occasionally on a weekend he would go into Browning and drink in the bars. Because of his size and status as a former marine, he became the favorite target of reservation toughs. A couple of times they ganged up on him and gave him some rough and tumble, but one-on-one I never heard of them getting the best of him. Fighting runs in our family.

A few years younger than John, my adopted brother Max became the 1955 Montana State Golden Gloves middleweight champion in boxing. He made it as far as the nationals in Chicago before being beaten by a black boxer. The coach of the Cut Bank Boxing Club, Larry Minckler, once saw Max knock the tar out of somebody. He convinced my folks of Max's potential as a boxer and apparently also spoke of the educational advantages Max would gain from attending a white school as opposed to the reservation high school. At the school, which I also attended, in the border town of Cut Bank, Max won a Heisey Award, became a football, track, and boxing standout, and was offered a boxing scholarship to Gonzaga University in the state of Washington. He married a white girl from Cut Bank, but her folks weren't happy with their daughter being married to an Indian, so the marriage didn't last long. After quitting college in his second year and returning to the reservation, Max continued boxing and started working on oil drilling rigs. At a large oil field outside Cut Bank, which has produced millions of gallons of oil since its discovery a half century ago, Max worked his way up to become a driller, a kind of boss of a drilling rig. Once while working in extremely cold weather – Cut Bank is often the coldest spot in the nation – high on a drilling rig, Max mashed his fingers between pieces of moving heavy metal. For six months he wore a fan-shaped cast on his hand while the bones healed. He had received an offer to turn pro boxer, but the drilling rig accident ended that hope. Max is the only member of my family alive today. He lives in Browning, and when I go home to visit, I sometimes stop at his house and we visit. He is twelve years my senior and knows stories from Cut Bank Creek that I haven't heard before. Sometimes we visit long. We're two, and we are left.

Quentin was ten years older than I, standing between Big John and Max in size – about six foot one, 190 pounds. Quentin was also a boxer and a street fighter; he and some of the locals would often get into fights with flyboys from the airbase outside of Cut Bank. He died at the age of twenty-two in 1958 from lung cancer, never having smoked a cigarette. At that time little was known about secondhand smoke. My folks both smoked.

I was adopted into a fighting family, a proud, complicated Blackfeet family that stood with one foot in the old ways and the other in the acculturated American ways. The profound changes experienced by the Blackfeet in the early reservation years reverberated deeply within individual families such as mine, affecting the relationships between fathers and sons. Apparently a deep attachment bound father to son in the pre-colonial days. A story in the ethnographic writings of the Blackfoot peoples tells of a man who would not give his son up to death; he carried the remains of the child with him for years in a travois behind his horse.

This tenderness was foreign to my father, who had turned to cow-boying after the buffalo culture was gone, and who had grown up immersed in the toughness of the American West. Such toughness or absence of sympathy seems to have become part of the western Indian male – and sometimes female – persona. Once when Big John was twelve, he and Max were returning from school on horseback, riding a big black gelding named Buick. Buick stepped into a badger hole and fell, hurting the boys badly. They were still crying when they came off the steep cutbank where the trail led down to the creek. Pop, watering horses on the far side of the creek, spied his sons crying. Rather than offering sympathy and comfort, he harshly ordered them to get to the house.

My pop, like so many Indians then and now, had *become* a cowboy. And something vital departed when that happened. The similarities between raising domestic cattle and hunting buffalo for Blackfeet pale when their differences are considered. The rituals associated with the running and killing of the buffalo were many; the horse was sacred; the buffalo was sacred; and the Grandmother, the Earth Spirit, was sacred. Cowboys are tough and work long, hard hours and ride dan-gerous horses for little pay, but they lack ritual, a sense of being part of something larger. The rituals of the Blackfoot Confederacy and other buffalo-hunting peoples offered a sense of spiritual connected-ness. Cattle kept the body alive for my Blackfeet family and others, but something essential was gone. Something existential. Something ontological. Something necessary.

We survived, then and now, our toughness not only making us prone to fighting and drinking but also helping us find ways to endure and to cope. When Joe and Isabell took me in at nine days of age in that cold

October of 1945, the deep snow and drifting wind made it impossible to travel even on horseback. As soon as the wind abated, my father and Big John, who had recently returned from active duty, saddled horses and went to hunt. They happened upon two bull elk that had followed Cut Bank Creek out of the mountains and onto the plains. (When the elk and deer can no longer get good feed near the mountains, hunger will usually drive them onto the plains. The animals will regularly follow one of the creeks that come out of the fastnesses of the mountains – Badger Creek, Two Medicine River, Cut Bank Creek, Birch Creek. These creeks are lined with cottonwood forests along their banks as they wend their way east to join the Big Muddy, the Missouri.) With the snowdrifts too deep to ride cross-country to Browning, some fifteen miles away, my diet those first days consisted solely of bull elk meat. My adopted mom would first chew the meat into a fine consistency and then feed it to me. In three or four days the ride to town was possible, and I once again had canned milk.

The knowledge that bull elk meat kept me alive as an infant has always been a part of my consciousness. I tend to see elk differently than others do, even if I have hunted and killed elk for food – all cow elk though and not the bull elk that helped me survive as an infant. One surely wouldn't want to kill one's medicine person. If I had screwed up by doing so, the old Pikuni would have said "he shit in his medicine sack."

Learning

My trail at four years old led to the town of Cut Bank, a white town, a border town. My folks had moved to a western town notorious for its overt racism toward Indians. Even though my folks had been taken away from the ceremonial aspects of Blackfoot life, in some senses we still lived as traditional Indians, hunting and gathering because we had no way of taking part in the economic life of Cut Bank. It was not comfortable there for an Indian. In the middle of the twentieth century, few Indian families lived in Cut Bank, maybe a dozen or so. Why they chose to live among the white people I do not know. We moved probably because my mother valued white education. Also, drinking was rampant on the reservation (alcohol was banned but bootlegging was common), and my mother never drank. Though we lived in Cut Bank, my full-blood father spent a lot of time in Browning, because for a two-year term, he was on the tribal council. I would ride the early morning no. 27 train with him from Cut Bank to Browning.

I was a spoiled child, or so I've been told, throwing tantrums when my mom refused to buy me something at a store. I was almost never spanked, yanked, shouted at, or roughly handled by my folks. Traditionally, Indian people didn't believe in corporal punishment for their children. My mom did hit me once, when I was six years old. In response to whatever I had or hadn't done on that particular six-year-old's morning, my mom grabbed my pop's long underwear and hit me with them. It's difficult to hurt someone with a pair of folded-over long underwear, but my mom said I screamed and cried as if I'd been hit with a cat-o'-nine-tails. That was the only physical discipline I received from my parents. My adopted brothers and sisters – Aurise, Katherine, John, Max, and Quentin – were, however, products of the world after the buffalo were gone, products of assimilation, and verily, verily, they did believe in a good thrashing. They knew how my mom felt about this, so they usually disciplined me when we were alone. My brothers and sisters acted more like surrogate parents – giving me a few good spankings – than siblings. But the spankings were few; I recall two spankings and one dunking. The old tribal wisdom was to throw cold water in the face of a small child when he was misbehaving. When I was about five or six years old, we camped at the annual powwow celebration in Browning. Because I was acting up, my folks permitted my brother Quentin to take me to the public pump and hold my head under the spigot while somebody else actuated the pump. The cold water immediately restored a sense of compliance with the orderly workings of the universe.

It is now 1951. I am taken to the Anna Jeffries School by my mom and left with Marjorie Hartman, the first grade teacher and principal, a woman with a severe demeanor who snaps her fingers so loudly it sounds like whips. When she wants quiet, her fingers snap, and instantly she has our attention. We try to make our fingers snap as loudly when we're on the playground but discover it is truly an art to produce that sharp cracking sound from one's fingertips. I cry inconsolably when my mom leaves me with this hard-looking white woman who can make me jump out of my skin with her electric fingers. I am the only dark-skinned child in the room.

Being the only Indian in a classroom soon became the norm as I worked my way through the grades at Anna Jeffries School. My white classmates got used to me. In the fourth grade another Indian boy, Wilson Guardipee, from the Blackfeet reservation joined the class. He was Indian and a stranger; I, however, had been there since first grade. The white boys dog piled him on the playground during recess; I suffered taunts now and then about my darkness. There wasn't anything either of us could do, except bear it. The issue of civil rights was in its infancy among blacks in the 1950s; among the Indians I knew, it just wasn't an issue.

I thus learned at an early age to relate with white people and their values. This knowledge has been both beneficial and harmful in my growth as a person and as an Indian through the years. I was lucky to have grown up with Indian people who weren't too far removed from the traditional culture, which has helped me in the world of academia. A lot of people my age didn't grow up with Blackfeet who were still hunting for subsistence, still drying meat and picking berries, and still speaking the language at home. My folks had spoken primarily Blackfeet in their youth and had spoken English as a second language, so their Anglo vocabulary was limited. But more than language, music formed the demarcation between the white and red worlds, and even between the half-blood and full-blood worlds. Every evening my pop would spread out an old army blanket, shuffle and deal his cards, and sing Blackfeet songs that must have come from a long way in the tribal distance. The tribal songs connect existentially; they are patterns of energy that allow immersion into the energies around us, telling us who we are. Eagle Shoe, unsympathetic cowboy that he was, still in many ways felt and practiced a connection to the earlier life, having been born about six years after the last Blackfeet buffalo hunt.

My biological mother, Lucille Monroe, drank too much and seemed to prefer white men. My biological father, as I've mentioned, left shortly after I was born and never returned. During my first thirteen years I would occasionally see her when she came to my folks' house; invariably she would be drunk and want me to give her a kiss. I kissed her without emotion. I think of her today and have a much better understanding of how she ended up alcoholic, how several generations of Indians have ended up alcoholic. I remember her crying to my mom once late at night. It seems that my biological father had sent Lucille – I had always known and will continue to know her as such – fifty dollars and asked that it be given to my mom, Isabell. Lucille instead drank up the only gift or assistance my father ever sent.

When I was in Mrs. Epstein's class in the second grade, Lucille and her current white man bought me a bicycle. They really wanted me to ride their present, but I didn't know how. It was fairly early in the morning, and they were probably just starting to get the day's drinking underway – drunks can be fun and entertaining at a certain stage, when they're feeling good, before they get boisterous and mean. On the sidewalk in front of my school, they made me try to ride the bike, over and over. After several attempts and spills, I noticed my classmates staring out the schoolroom window at me, taking in the strange spectacle of their dark-skinned cohort flopping unceremoniously onto the sidewalk while two adults laughed at his feeble attempts. I just couldn't ride the bike, and with my classmates as onlookers, it became impossible to even try. I started crying and finally was allowed to go back to my classroom.

That image remains one of the strongest memories of my young life.

I was humiliated again a year later in Mrs. Dusek's class. Like many Indians, especially Indian children, I was extremely shy. One day my shyness initially prevented me from approaching the teacher and requesting to go to the bathroom. Soon, however, I was desperate and approached Mrs. Dusek, but she refused. Back in the chair, my body soon took over. A girl sitting across from me looked at the piss running onto the floor toward her. Raising her feet and hand, she announced there was a puddle of water on the floor, approaching her desk.

Oh, the shame of it all.

Roland Kjose, who lived across the street from the school, was sent to bring a pair of his trousers for me. Mrs. Dusek is now probably long dead. I hope the Lord makes her daily wade through a lake of piss plumb to her armpits for the embarrassment she caused me.

It was in the fifth grade that I first was jolted into the awareness that the little barbs about dark skin and about being an Indian were not limited to my classmates – adults also were very much concerned with the color of a person's skin and all of the implications that went with it. A hundred yards from the playground was the playing field of the American Legion baseball team. We discovered that the dugouts, carrying the secrecy of their below-ground atmosphere, were wonderful places to invite girls. Karen Hoff took a liking to me, and we flirted merrily with each other. She apparently told her mom about her attachment to me. Her mother, associating the Kipp name with Indian because my boxer brother Max was getting lots of press then, told her daughter that she would be disowned and not allowed in the house again if she ever married an Indian. Karen reported this startling news to me.

That particular incident proved to be my entrance into the world of white supremacy in America. A few years hence along my trail I would come to realize, sadly, that Mrs. Hoff's attitude was not an aberration. America was built on that attitude. It had leaped off the ship with Columbus.

It always brings a little sharp pain, and probably always will, whenever I hear stories of children of color confronting racism for the first time in America. It always hurts.

My best friend for a few years was a white kid named Brian Neidhardt who lived across the street from me. I was about ten when my folks moved into his neighborhood, and for the next several years we were inseparable. He called my folks mom and pop the same way I did. Staying at his house overnight gave me insight into how white people lived and thought. Brian's biological parents had separated when he was still a child and both had remarried. His mother did believe in corporal punishment, and he was amazed that I never received thrashings the way he did. Eventually Brian's biological father let it be known that it wasn't a good thing for his son to be hanging around with an Indian. Our bond of boyhood was soon gone. By the time we entered high school, Brian's and my wild, free boyhood days were over, and we found different friends to hang around.[1]

Not all white adults disliked Indians. Bob Durham, a white county extension agent or some such at the courthouse, befriended my pop. Bob's son was my age, and we got along well. Although he lived in a very distinctly middle-class setting on the south side of town, he would come to my house and I would go to his. My being Indian didn't seem to bother the Durham family. I often ate with them.

My first six years of school would probably have been a little easier if it had been known that I was quite blind. The problem first became apparent to others in the fall of my seventh grade. As usual, I was hunting with my pop and my older brothers, this time tracking deer and pheasants on the bottomlands of Birch Creek in the southern part of the Blackfeet reservation. Chinese pheasants had been imported some years before and now thrived in the grain fields and irrigation ditches that cover that part of the reservation. Figuring it was time for me to learn how to shoot a shotgun, Eagle Shoe handed me the shotgun without explanation and with only a quick forward nod of his head. I took the gun and pushed the safety off, trying to see what he saw.

I couldn't see anything. Abruptly a rooster pheasant took flight. "Why didn't you shoot?" my pop asked. "I couldn't see it," I admitted. He was incredulous; the rooster had only been about forty feet distant and in plain sight. My mother took me to the eye doctor, and we learned that I was very nearsighted. After getting glasses, I was amazed by the starry night sky. Nobody wore glasses in the old days; a warrior wouldn't last long if his sight was deficient.

Despite my physical blindness, by the seventh grade I began to see some things more clearly. I began to understand that Cut Bank was divided – the north side was where the lower working class, unemployed, and Indians lived. Also living there was a family named Kubis, who were known as DPs (displaced persons), from Poland, I believe. They looked like regular old white people to me, but the other whites somehow considered them tainted. The Kubis family, very white and blond, remained a mystery: why did white people in the town put them down?

Being Indian helped me flunk seventh grade. My folks, neither having attended high school, didn't understand the importance of homework and how a white educational system functioned. Getting me up and off to school was their duty; the schoolteachers in turn were responsible for teaching. While my white boyhood friends stayed in and did their homework, I would take off for Cut Bank Creek and play along the river. Once, a seventh grade teacher named Leo Sherrod became upset because I didn't turn in the required homework in a math class. Standing over me, he asked why I didn't think it was important to hand in the work. I shrugged my shoulders, and he slapped me hard across the face. I told my mom, but no action was taken, to my knowledge – my boxing brother Max was never told. Though there was very little talk of racism in our house, it lurked just beneath the surface. For me to be slapped by a white teacher implicated the larger issue of family honor.[2] Leo Sherrod is probably an old man by now, but if I were ever to see that white man, I would disregard his advanced years and thrash him good for slapping me the way he did. I know, vengeance is mine saith the Lord, but I'd beg the Lord, just this once, to let me have firsts.

A few swift blows to the rear with a garden hose followed the slap. Some girl in my seventh grade class apparently took a liking to me, scratching my name into a desk in one of the classrooms. Although the desks bore many marks of graffiti from previous years, seldom did anyone have the audacity to put their own name on the desk. One day I was told to report to the principal's office immediately. The principal was Miss Skaw, who wore very thick glasses, pulled her hair into a tight bun, and was the housemate of my first grade teacher, Miss Hartman (there were allegations of lesbianism, but I don't believe anyone knew for sure). Miss Skaw asked me why I had written my name on a school desk. Perplexed, I retorted that I had not done so. Having seen for herself the inscribed name, Woody Kipp, she inquired if another Woody Kipp also attended the Cut Bank junior high school. Confused by this wrongful accusation, all I could do was admit that there was only one Woody Kipp in the school. She then lectured me. "Those desks cost money, the taxpayers of this county, including me, pay for those desks, and we don't like it one bit that nitwits like you mark them all up so we have to pay for repairs to the desks." Reaching into a desk drawer, Miss Skaw drew out a piece of rubber garden hose, about eighteen inches in length. I was forced to bend over and was struck a half dozen times on the rear.

Feeling wrongly convicted, I told some of my classmates what had happened. The tale passed quickly from student to student in the junior high classes. The enamored girl – whoever she was – must have heard what had happened as a result of her crush on me; wrestling with her conscience for some time, she eventually admitted to the deed. When school began the following fall – my second year as a seventh grader – I was once again told to report to Miss Skaw's office. Approaching her office with dread, not knowing what to expect this time, I was met with a smile and the truth. As a reward, I was chosen to be the student who collected tardy slips from classroom to classroom and delivered messages between the teachers and the administration.

During those years I learned to read and write but heard nothing of the deep metaphysical teachings that were my heritage; I was taught nothing of actual North American history, except from a Eurocentric point of view. By the seventh grade, I didn't know who I really was or where I had come from; in my mind, George Washington was my ethnical grandfather. I entered an essay contest, wrote my submission on that topic, and lost. The winner, Layla Smith (the smartest girl in the class), told me that she overheard two teachers in the lounge saying I had actually won but they gave it to Layla because I was an Indian. The teachers *knew* that I wasn't an ethnical grandson of

George Washington, that I'd been hoodwinked by their version of history; they gave the prize instead to a more appropriate descendant, a white girl.

When my seventh grade civics teacher, Miss Montague, talked of my people, whose border was only a mile away, she called them Pieguns, and I never blinked an eye. What she meant was Piegans, the whites' incorrect name for us. Our name, as I have said, is Pikuni. *Pee-ku-nee*; the *ku* sounds like cut. Piegan, pronounced *pay-gan*, poured forth from Miss Montague's lips as pie and guns. Pieguns. I didn't have any idea what she was talking about. I thought she meant pagans, whoever they were. I had grown up hearing my folks use the term Piegan but the white woman pronounced the word in such a strange fashion I didn't recognize she was referring to my own people.

For a Pagan, I guess the Catholic Church rested rather deeply in me. The summer going into eighth grade, the town of Cut Bank started a Little League baseball program. My age allowed me to play for one year. At the same time, my godmother, Aurise, arranged for me to go to catechism school at the local Catholic church, where I would receive my first communion. I've often thought about that admixture of baseball and church in the summer of my twelfth year. There was some kind of lesson in it. In Little League I played on a team called the Prairie Dogs, coached by a man named Earl Sturm, who had played semi-pro ball in his youth. Our twenty-five-game schedule proved to be a long season; we lost twenty-four games and won one. In one of the games, we squared off against the Hawks, who were coached by a rancher named Don Weaver and who ended up winning twenty-four games and losing one. You guessed it. We were the team who beat the Hawks, and I pitched the game. The last shall be first or some such from the Bible – a strange play of religion and baseball in my twelfth year.

I was thirteen when my biological mother died at the age of forty-three from too much whiskey. At her funeral in Browning, I did not cry. I knew very little about Lucille Monroe.

Becoming

The year I entered Cut Bank High School, an Indian girl named Dixie committed an amazing number of immoral acts. Or so it was said. Dixie was poor and lived on the north side of the tracks on a certain squalid block that housed many Indians coming directly off the Blackfeet Indian reservation. A lot of drinking went on in that quarter.

Dixie left after a year and never returned. Although only about fifteen, she allegedly engaged in all sorts of deeds of ill repute, acts no white girl would have dreamed of doing. How the white boys could have known such things about her, I didn't know. Dixie would have been awfully busy to have lived up to her reputation. Today, I understand that she was a victim of what the literary theorists call othering, ascribing unfavorable attitudes and behaviors to the Other, who is not white.

Basketball prevented me from being othered. My advantage over Dixie and some of the other Indian students was my proficiency at a non-Indian sport; I made the varsity basketball team in my sophomore year. The coach was an ex-marine officer named Willie DeGroot, whose guidance and advice proved invaluable during my high school years. I also became a shot-putter on the track team. I have never been very heavy, weighing some 165 pounds then, but I have always been wiry. When I was a junior, I took second at the divisional track meet in shot put, throwing against some very big, stout farm boys. I hoped to win it in my senior year.

Over the next three years, I was academically just good enough to remain on the sports teams. Basketball was an incentive to get passing grades. I was far from the model academic student in high school, but I did read. My parents were elderly, we didn't own a television, and so I read a lot. While the English teachers were explaining how to diagram sentences, I was reading Hemingway's *Death in the Afternoon*, Irving Stone's *The Agony and the Ecstasy*, the horrific Civil War novel *Andersonville* by MacKinlay Kantor, and Kyle Onstott's *Mandingo*. I sought out the latter book because I'd overheard men discussing the book's sexual content. The interracial sex between the young "master" of the plantation and the black women and, ultimately, between his white wife and the huge fighting Mandingo was provocative subject matter for me. The book's attitudes toward such taboo intermingling soon hit home.

Though most students accepted me for my sports skills, the intolerance of adults outside of school continued. In the spring of my sophomore year, while at a local outdoor drive-in theater with some friends and a case of beer, I ended up in the back seat of a car making out with a tall blonde named Linda Barney. For the next month or so we were a regular couple, at least at the drive-in theater. Linda, like Karen Hoff, eventually informed me that our relationship extremely displeased her mother. Another lesson in how the American Dream was being realized in Cut Bank, Montana. Linda's mother had more than me to worry about, though. By the next fall, Linda had gotten pregnant by some white guy who had shown up during the summer months while I was away working on a ranch. She went away to have the baby and returned the next year.

Not learning from the sad example of my biological mother, I began to drink frequently in high school. Why are Native peoples so susceptible to the influence of alcohol? Nobody has come up with a single satisfactory answer. Sociologists, scientists, and counselors from many camps have advanced theories ranging from the premise of a missing gene or enzyme to the uncontestable fact that Natives haven't had the same long period of opportunity as Europeans to evolve physically in order to deal with the effects of alcohol. The receptivity of many Blackfeet to alcohol is also bound up with their adoption of values associated with the toughness of cowboy life. And there's the self-esteem explanation: feeling inferior in the face of the advanced technology, military might, and cultural domination of whites, Indians took to the bottle. Whatever the reason – physical, moral, spiritual, physiological – Indians cannot use liquor with any amount of reason, especially full-bloods. It seems to me that the more Indian blood one has, the less one is able to handle alcohol. Indians are mostly pacific when sober; the rate of reservation crimes revolving around alcohol use and abuse, however, is absolutely astounding. A few years ago, a graduate student studied the incarceration of Native men at the Montana State Penitentiary. Ninety-five percent of the Indian men locked up there had committed their crime while drunk.

One night during the Christmas holidays of my junior year, I nearly killed myself while drinking. A friend had obtained a quart of Everclear liquor, and I drank nearly a whole water glass full, not knowing that it was two hundred proof. It's a wonder my heart didn't stop. I lost my glasses and don't remember my friend taking me home. My mom and pop helped my friend get me to bed, as I was passed out in his car. I slept through the 9:00 a.m. basketball practice and woke up with a terrible hangover. About 9:30 a.m. coach DeGroot came by and escorted me to the gymnasium. Although a drinker himself, the coach had a serious talk with me about alcohol after the practice was over. His advice didn't sink in; later that year several of us were kicked off the team for drinking. The members of the team who hadn't been caught drinking, however, were allowed to decide whether the banishment would be permanent. They voted instead to retain us.

My proficiency in sports was accepted more readily than my ability in the classroom. In my junior year, despite my protests to the contrary, one of my teachers accused me of plagiarism, claiming that I had borrowed heavily from a magazine article when writing an essay for her class. Misunderstanding across the racial divide reared its ugly head again. My teacher could not accept that an Indian could actually write, could actually engage with complex ideas rather than simply work or play sports with their hands. There are some things that Indians say or want to say that white people don't understand.

During my senior year my world changed further. I'd been given fifteen dollars to defray traveling expenses while playing in an independent Indian basketball tournament on the Blackfeet reservation, which was after the conclusion of the regular high school season. I was considered to have accepted money for athletics and was thus disqualified from participating in track my senior year. The news got worse. About a month and a half before graduation in 1964, the high school counselor informed me that I was a half credit short in English. Rather than return to school that fall for half of the year, I dropped out. My mom must have been quite disappointed when I didn't graduate, but, typical of her, she didn't criticize me. Late that spring I moved to my folks' ranch, run by my brother Big John, and began farming for him.

When coach DeGroot heard the news, he drove the twenty-six miles from Cut Bank to our farm-ranch on Cut Bank Creek to encourage me to return to school that fall. The coach believed he could get me a basketball scholarship to Carrol College, a Catholic school in Helena. He felt I wasn't big enough to play at the major universities but thought I might do well at a smaller school. The thought of playing more basketball sounded inviting. I considered it. I also began considering something else.

My family held the Marine Corps in great esteem; Big John and my high school coach had been marines. Just outside the doors of the Glacier County courthouse hung a Marine Corps poster about four feet high; the marine looked dazzling to me in his dress blues. But Big John, who had also dropped out of high school, warned me against joining.

"Why don't you join the Air Force?" he would say. "You'll learn a trade. The Marine Corps won't teach you nothing." I wasn't convinced. Although a learned trade would have benefited a high school dropout, I was eighteen years old and convinced that war was glamorous.

The other option would be to work on our ranch on Cut Bank Creek. For more than a century the U.S. governmental agencies have been trying to get former buffalo hunters to become farmers, with mixed results at best. One of the stipulations of the last Blackfeet treaty, the Agreement of 1895, states specifically that those Indians who pursued agriculture would be rewarded above and beyond others. In 1964 Big John had been managing a successful farming enterprise for about ten years. Overseeing my folks' allotted land of two thousand acres in the heart of the Blackfeet Indian Reservation, he was the largest Blackfoot farmer on the reservation (maybe our distant cousin Roy Allison, who lived outside the reservation, farmed a larger piece; maybe not). Big John lived his whole life – except for the time spent in the Marine Corps – on that piece of ground.

Big John and his second wife, Mildred, whom we called Bobby, worked very hard. Bobby would get up at 5:00 a.m.; by 6:00 we would have eaten breakfast and be heading for the plowing fields. When the tractor was readied by 7:30 a.m., there was nothing left to do but get into the seat and lower the shovels into Mother Earth and start plowing.

Big John owned a 1951 3/4-ton Chevy that was indispensable for farm work. It hauled a 120-gallon tank of diesel fuel for the tractors, grease in 5-gallon buckets, grease guns that were filled from the buckets, oil filters for the tractors, water cans in case the radiators were low, gasoline for the "little joe" starting engine, which warmed the tractor before I threw the dual switches that shifted the engine from warming up on gas to diesel, shovels for the plows, hand tools to change the shovels, hydraulic oil for the system used to lift the plow out of the ground, and hydraulic hoses in case a hose broke. His tractors were used but usable. I summer fallowed or plowed with an International WD-9 wheel tractor and a TD-9 crawler tractor, more commonly know as a cat. Our equipment was fairly small compared to some of the big non-Indian farmers who farmed close by. Chet Sammons, a white farmer who bordered our property, owned massive tractors and plows. [1]

Grinding monotony. Summer fallowing is dreary work – up one side of a wind strip and down the other, all day, up and back, monotony piling upon monotony. The drone of the diesel engines was the only thing I heard for hours on end. We had no power steering in those days, no radios or air conditioning either. Because of the high winds on that part of the plains, the strip farming method was employed, planting one strip of land approximately a hundred yards wide while the next hundred-yard strip lay fallow. The fallow strips would be plowed several times in the spring and summer to kill the weeds, aerate the soil, and retain the moisture. The strips varied in length, some being more than a mile in length while some were much shorter, depending upon the terrain being farmed and the location of the allotment pins. [2]

I found driving the wheel tractor not as noisy and rough as the cat, but it was more dangerous. Rocks as big around and thick as a washtub were thickly deposited across parts of the farmland. When the front wheels of the wheel tractor hit those rocks, it would cause the steering wheel to spin instantly – if your fingers or wrists were caught by the whirling steering wheel, it really hurt. It wasn't wise to wear a watch while plowing. Some farmers picked the rocks out of the fields by using a hydraulic lifting system, which was fitted on the front of the tractor. It's time-consuming, however, to remove several thousands of acres of rocks. And they keep coming back. When you've picked the field clear of the big rocks, after a plowing or two they come out of the ground again. On our ranch, we picked rocks for a while and then gave up.

We would plow till the sun went down. (I wish I had a videotape of one of our working days to show to white people who chant their mantra about lazy Indians.) We plowed till sundown, went home and ate, retired to bed by 10:00 p.m., and then woke up the next morning and did it again. This routine was often accompanied by a roar. The caterpillar's steel tracks and cleats created a loud noise when crossing fields covered with rocks. My ears would ring with the roar of steel on rock for hours afterward, continuing even when I went to bed.

As that exhausting, deafening summer of 1964 dragged on, the poster marine in dress blues beckoned more invitingly. In early June, a few days before we were drenched with days of rain, which resulted in a major flood that cost thirty-nine people their lives, Big John sent me to Cut Bank to get a piece of machinery from one of the farm implement businesses. After concluding my farm duties I drove to the courthouse and inquired about the schedule of the Marine Corps recruiter. I was lucky; an elderly white woman in one of the county offices pointed out the recruiter just down the hallway from her office.

During the next hour, I left one trail and began another, which would twist and turn far away from the reservation and on to foreign shores but eventually would lead me back. I signed up to be in Butte, Montana, on July 13, 1964, for induction into the United States Marine Corps.[3]

Leaving

4

I was not the first person in my family to serve in the U.S. military. Long before Big John joined the marines, my great-uncle William Jackson – grandson of Hugh Munro – scouted for General Custer. His father, a white man, had lost his job at Fort Benton, in Montana Territory, because of changing political winds. Fort Benton was the spot where trade goods and annuity goods that were owed to the Indians were taken off the Missouri River and loaded onto bull trains; goods also went to the gold fields of Montana. My great-uncle's father, upon losing his position, built a keelboat, loaded his family and worldly goods, and floated eastward to Fort Buford in present-day North Dakota, where he knew the man running the trading post; he was hired. His two sons, ages seventeen and nineteen, joined a local band of young Arikaras who were scouting for Custer.

I took the first steps on the new trail in a 1957 Ford given to me by my mother during my senior year in high school. On my way to Cut Bank a tire went flat, however, and since the spare was also flat, I hitchhiked to Cut Bank, parking the Ford off the road. Big John towed the vehicle back to the ranch.[1] Boarding a bus in Cut Bank, I left for Butte and found myself a couple of days later at the Marine Corps recruit depot in San Diego. I was chewing gum when the Marine Corps drill instructor showed up at the San Diego airport to pick us up. He told me to spit the gum out. I hesitated – it seemed a strange request. In a moment, the DI jammed his finger in my mouth, yelling that I was a lowlife civilian scumbag piece of shit. The guy wasn't fooling, and he had the power to back up what he was saying.

Despite the incident at the airport, I went through boot camp fairly easily. I was used to a big booming voice telling me what to do and how to do things. Big John had been a disciplinarian on the ranch, and in the forest hunting, and on the lakes trapping beaver. During the thirteen weeks of boot camp and the month of intense infantry training at Camp Pendleton, California, I began to hear increasingly of a faraway place called Vietnam. Although the drill instructors had made it clear that we marines might be called into the conflict, I didn't really consider the possibility imminent.

Following boot camp and infantry training, I was ordered to report to Camp LeJeune in North Carolina after a month's furlough. Wanting to see the country, I decided to cross the continent to Camp LeJeune by bus. I checked into LeJeune in mid-December. Because I was to become a combat engineer, Military Occupational Specialty 1345, I was sent immediately to Cherry Point and began instruction in the operation of heavy equipment. Apparently my experience driving heavy farm equipment helped qualify me for the USMC heavy equipment engineer school.

I did the usual tack as a marine while in LeJeune – drinking on weekends, fighting, getting thrown into the drunk tank. In the early part of 1965, while still attending the engineer school, I was told to report to the docks with a TD-15 dozer and to standby to go to the Dominican Republic, the scene of some kind of insurrection. I soon boarded a landing ship tank – no. 1163, if I remember correctly – and sailed around the Dominican Republic for thirty-six days. There were pieces of real war machinery on the ship, like a tracked vehicle with 106 Recoilless rifles sticking out of the front of it, six barrels in all, a deadly piece of machinery. I never unloaded my piece of equipment.

When the rebellion reached a stalemate, we sailed back to LeJeune and I completed my engineer training.

During my time in LeJeune I began to learn an important lesson about racial relations and the depth of hatred and misunderstanding in 1960s America. I made friends with two black guys, one named Tavaras and the other named Jesse. Growing up in the all-white town of Cut Bank had given me certain ideas about black people. My black friends taught me otherwise, a lesson as much about myself as them. I once overheard Jesse talking to another black and using the term "splib dude." When I asked him what a splib was, he replied that it stood for Segregated People Living in Brotherhood.

I soon better understood my black friends' affinity with me. Indians serving in the military on the East Coast were somewhat of a rarity. Fueled by nostalgic and inaccurate stereotypes of Indians, which were perpetuated by western movies and other media, the white marines often saw me as a historical oddity, firing the same inane questions in my direction that Indians continue to be asked in the twenty-first century: Do you live in a tipi? Do you ride horses and hunt buffalo? It would have been more to the point if they had asked: Do you fuck, fight, and flagellate against the powers of the world without the benefit of the true way?

One cold February morning in 1965, a half dozen marines and I were standing around warming ourselves from a diesel-lit fire in a fifty-five-gallon barrel. As usual at such times, we smoked, drank coffee, and told crude marine jokes. This morning would be different. A white marine appeared around the corner of a building, hollering, "Hey, they just shot and killed Malcolm X!" Whoops of joyous camaraderie greeted his news. "Good for that big-mouth black motherfucker!" one of the other marines exclaimed.

Not political or well informed about racial relations at that time, I was taken aback by the laughing vehemence at the death of a black man. That laughter would linger and take on deeper meaning. Over the next decade I would come to see why the white marines celebrated the death of Malcolm X and, at a place called Wounded Knee, why a military response might seem a viable way to deal with the ravages of white society. The cultural brothers of those marines warming their hands at a diesel fire in North Carolina had much to learn about the inalienable rights of all Americans.

There was another leaving during this time of my life. Shortly after returning from the Dominican Republic I was notified that my father, Eagle Shoe, had died. He had been placed in a nursing home for the last few months of his life. On a thirty-day furlough, I began a journey back to the reservation for my father's funeral. Along the way home I stopped at Great Falls, Montana, to visit briefly with a high school friend, Sandy Harrington. Possessing Indian blood but not visibly Indian, Sandy had returned from back East during my junior year of high school. We had sat by each other in one class, and though there never was anything other than an implied relationship, we kept in contact through letters when I was in boot camp, and she continued to write as I went through the engineer school. Sandy agreed to meet me at the Greyhound bus depot in Great Falls just before I was scheduled to head north to the reservation at 5:00 p.m.

I arrived in Great Falls with most of the morning and all of the afternoon to wait, so I decided to try to get served in a bar (I was nineteen, and the drinking age was twenty-one). I got served. After drinking a few beers, dressed in a winter green marine uniform, I went to another bar and started a conversation with a white airman from Malstrom Air Base on the outskirts of Great Falls. Our conversation was initially congenial but soon turned nasty as we debated the merits of our respective services. Because the drill instructors at San Diego thoroughly indoctrinated me into the superiority of marines, we were soon locked in a heated debate. I remember the airman saying, as he rose from his barstool and headed for the restroom, "You fucking marines are crazier than hell." When he emerged from the men's room, he called out to me from where he stood by a shuffleboard – "Hey, jarhead, want to play a game of shuffleboard?" Still pissed at our earlier conversation, I replied, "No, I don't fucking play with pussies."

In a few moments I learned another one of life's major lessons: if you're going to call somebody a pussy, you better keep your eye on them. I was sitting there acting tough after talking tough when suddenly my bar stool was spun around and I caught a hard right in the nose. Blood squirting down the front of my uniform, I first was more concerned about Uncle Sam's uniform getting bloody than my broken nose (that still bothers me to this day). The blow knocked me to the floor, and the guy threw a couple of kicks at me, but I regained my wits enough to block his kicks. When I started to get up, the flyboy panicked and tore for the door. I almost caught him as he pulled the door open, but he managed to get out into the street and run. The whole front of my uniform splattered with blood, I chased him for about a half block and then gave up. An elderly barmaid was sympathetic and helped clean my uniform as best she could with napkins from the bar.

It was late in the afternoon, so I left the bar and went to the Greyhound bus depot to meet Sandy Harrington. My nose was swollen; I gingerly felt it and realized it was broken, as I could move it around. The bus from Helena pulled in, and I was getting ready to get on, when Sandy finally showed up. My broken nose had swelled to such proportions that she at first didn't recognize me. After we visited for a brief ten minutes, the bus pulled out for Cut Bank. I would never see Sandy Harrington again, though I kept her high school picture in my military wall locker for quite some time afterward.

During the two-hour bus ride from Great Falls to Cut Bank, I made the acquaintance of a young, slim Blackfoot named Irving "Tooky Man" Spotted Eagle. The nickname Tooky Man is a corruption of the Blackfoot word for drum – *istookuman*. He was on his way home after doing a stint in Cleveland learning to be a welder. Little did I know at the time that there was something prescient in our meeting – I had just lost my father, and in a few years Irving's father, Sam Spotted Eagle, would become my surrogate father, bringing an understanding of the sacred, teaching the meanings of the Sacred Pipe, and revealing the nuances of becoming a leader of a Sweat Lodge ceremony.[2]

Following my father's funeral, I stayed on the Blackfeet reservation for the remainder of my thirty-day furlough, working as a roughneck on an oil rig with my brother Max. The work was hard, dangerous, and bitterly cold. Max ran the controls that lowered the long lengths of drill pipe into position; the rest of us used chains and big wrenches to hook the drill pipe to the pipe already in the ground. The giant diesel engine would then be revved up as the new pipe disappeared into the ground in search of black gold.

The money was good during that brief time back home, and I tied back in with some of my high school friends who were still in Cut Bank. We partied; being a marine gave me a certain prominence. We heard that Pete Jensen, a bully who had been a year ahead of me in school, had been in Vietnam already and had been shot in the buttocks while in a helicopter. The friends I partied with thought it quite funny that Pete had been shot in the ass. For me, Vietnam was becoming more real.

Fighting

After finishing the engineer school, I became a working member of the Second Marine Division. In June 1965 I received orders to report to Camp Pendleton, California, to prepare to go overseas. Although we were going to Japan, Vietnam remained very much on my mind. Reports of fighting trickled in, and being newly trained marines, we were eager to hear any news of combat. Looking back, I must admit that nineteen-year-old men don't know enough about life to be sent to a war; they don't have sufficient respect for life to be sent with weapons of mass destruction among women and children.

We boarded the troop ship USS *General Mitchell*, which held some three thousand marines plus about five hundred sailors. We were advised that along the way we would be given overnight liberty in Honolulu. The marine chaplain, in sessions we were required to attend, warned us about venereal disease and advised against frequenting Hotel Street in Honolulu, a district full of bars and hookers. Of course, upon disembarking, our dicks as hard as iron, we headed immediately for Hotel Street.

Returning to the dock sometime after midnight, a group of us went to a restaurant that was partly out into the harbor. Having bought pints of whiskey before leaving the bars on Hotel Street, some of us were good and drunk by the time we reached the restaurant. A group of sailors sat at the bar, and inevitably interservice taunts flew back and forth until a full-fledged fight exploded. I traded punches with a sailor near the railing of the restaurant, a few feet above the water. He hit me hard up the side of the head and my glasses – my only pair – tumbled into the dark waters of the harbor. Though now half blind, I continued fighting, getting in some good punches – I was a Kipp after all. The shore patrol soon appeared, blowing whistles and bringing the brawl to a halt. The next morning we left Honolulu; I was hung over, sore from getting punched, and mostly blind. Replacement glasses weren't available on the ship; I would need to wait until we reached Japan.

About two days out from Honolulu, our ship was sliced by the edge of a hurricane. The ocean swells became massive, and soon we weren't allowed out on deck. While the ship tossed and waves crashed over the deck topside, we were confined to sleeping quarters for two days, stacked in tiers of six tiny cots. The turbulence made nearly everybody seasick. Marines, hundreds of them, vomited all over the place – it was rank. At one point I was so seasick that if the ship had begun sinking I probably wouldn't have even moved from the cot.

At last reaching Yokohama, Japan, we were given evening liberty. I found the beautiful Japanese girls intoxicating; my head swam with visions of partaking of such pulchritude for the next year.

Hung over, the next morning I was greeted with fearful, exciting news – our orders had changed. We would not be going to the marine airbase at Iwakuni but instead would be boarding the USS *Navarro* at Okinawa, which would take us to the Republic of South Vietnam. For many of my fellow marines, the USS *Navarro* would be their penultimate journey; the final trip would be a sad return home in body bags. It would take decades for me to comprehend the strange, deranged, and evil things that transpired in the name of justice and democracy when I was in Vietnam.

As we sailed toward Vietnam, images and scenarios tumbled in my mind – marines storming a beach with machine gun fire making the water boil, men dying in the surf. What the drill instructors had hinted darkly of in boot camp and the infantry training regiment took root. I was as excited as much as I was scared – I certainly didn't want to die, but as a teenager I was also lured by the thrilling and chilling prospect of engaging the enemy with guns. However, neither action nor enemy greeted us when we eventually disembarked on a Vietnamese beach under a hot, mid-September sun and under the watchful eyes of a marine company on the lookout for snipers. We went ashore quietly and unharmed and were driven to a compound near the Da Nang airbase, where we would spend our tour in Vietnam.

I had been assigned to the support unit of Marine Air Group Eleven. Our job was to support the grunts fighting in the field; our pilots dropped bombs and napalm, shot rockets, and strafed with machine guns. They flew the F-4B Phantom fighter-bomber, a constant roar that continues to echo through the years. Sometimes at night, as I lie in bed, the roar and whine of death again lifts off into the sky. Sometimes it's odd not to hear that sound. Those Phantoms are like a girlfriend who after a bitter argument leaves for good. I don't miss her, but the apartment seems strange without her.

We were combat engineers – in civilian terms, heavy equipment operators – who were required to carry an M-14 with two full twenty-round magazines of ammunition on whatever piece of equipment we were operating. As part of the first major troop buildup in Vietnam, we worked day and night for the first six months constructing the infrastructure around the Da Nang airbase. A graduate from the heavy equipment school, I was licensed to run all of the heavy equipment in our unit, including rough terrain forklifts, bulldozers, truck-mounted cranes, road graders, front-end loaders, hydraulic cranes, drag lines, and small forklifts that could be disassembled into six pieces and carried by choppers to airfields that were cut into the jungles. I had reached Vietnam without eyeglasses – damn that sailor – and would have been in tough shape had I been a grunt. During the two weeks it took to acquire a new pair of eyeglasses, I couldn't operate any heavy equipment, so I assisted the mechanics at the heavy equipment lot and helped maintain the forklifts and cranes that were being used day and night to load bombs for the F-4B Phantom fighter-bombers.

It began to rain not long after we arrived. And it rained, and it rained, and it rained. Thirteen inches fell in the first few days after the monsoons began, the equivalent of a year's rainfall back home. The rain would vary from a warm, steady drizzle to a drenching torrent, but it never completely abated. I can imagine what it must have been like fighting in the jungles in the rain; it was bad enough operating heavy equipment all day and sometimes all night without getting a chance to dry out.

We were not on the front lines, but the war went on around us. The Phantoms continually took off from the runway laden with death, and artillery shells exploded in the mountains around us, occasionally hitting the airfield. Not long after we arrived, a plane was hit by gunfire and crashed into a village at the end of the runway, incinerating people, pigs, chickens, and houses. I was sent with a front-end loader to help clean up the mess. Nearly every night and sometimes all night long illumination flares would flash and gunfire would erupt along the perimeter of the airfield as the grunts on guard duty fired into the darkness at real and perceived threats. Such proximity to combat did not satisfy some of us, like my friend John Pinkerton from Akron, Ohio, who, succumbing to the romantic, adventurous lure of the Marine Corps legends, wanted to leave the engineers behind and fight with the grunts in the mountains and jungles.

I was the only Indian in our outfit, and I went by the generic name of Chief. Today there are Indians in the military who resist this name being applied to them, but it didn't bother me then, as I was proud to be an Indian and glad that others knew it. Ignorance, not malevolence, prompted the title.

Like many other Indians in Vietnam, I was surprised at our physical resemblance to the Vietnamese people – brown skin, black hair. My biological mother was Oriental-looking; her nickname on the Blackfeet reservation had been Shanghai, and I inherited her Oriental-looking eyes. The Vietnamese scrutinized me, wondering how I had come to look so like them, though bigger. *You same same Viet Cong*. My fellow marines pointedly brought this resemblance to my attention during my first incarceration in the Third Marine Amphibious Force brig in the early part of 1967. After getting to know one of the black marines while on a hard-labor working detail, he told me a story about myself. The marine had been standing with another black guy named Jones somewhere inside the brig gate when they had brought me in. "Well, I told my bro Jones," he confessed, "lookee there, Jones, there's the biggest motherfuckin' Chinaman I ever did see." The Vietnamese didn't seem so strange to me. I would listen to them talking in Vietnamese and wish I could speak with them and ask questions about their lives. The white soldiers, however – like white soldiers from the time of Columbus and probably even long before ol' Chris came bouncing over the waves in his little wooden tubs – cursed the dark-skinned people as being inferior. They were sure of an ultimate victory, as Uncle Sam, with the exception of the Little Bighorn in 1876, hadn't lost too many battles.

Alcohol accompanied us overseas. The Marine Corps in my experience promoted an environment that glamorized drinking and made it integral to the persona of a marine – drinking and toughness were twins I came to know well. After two weeks of receiving two hot beers in the evenings, we heard exciting news one afternoon from Staff Sergeant Smith, a tall, lanky, mustachioed lifer from the Deep South. A refrigeration unit had been hooked up at the far northern end of the hooches, and we would be able to drink as much beer as we wanted that evening, from 6:00 p.m. till 10:00 p.m. We went en masse and started drinking as soon as duty permitted. Another Smith, Gunnery Sergeant Smith – a little, loudmouthed marine who was always talking about his exploits in the Korean War but who one time left us stranded with heavy equipment out in the bush when machine guns went off nearby – warned us to go easy on the beer. If the Viet Cong were to attempt to overrun the airbase, we would have to go to our defensive positions on the perimeter; if we were drunk that night, Victor Charlie would find it easier to kill us. We listened to Smith's harangue but drank recklessly, soon becoming involved in a major drunken scrap with marines from the motor transport platoon (who were actually part of the same organization that we were).

The old marine's warning proved true. A couple of marines on guard duty at the end of the airstrip, who had apparently gone to sleep on guard duty that night, were found garroted with a piece of fine wire; in downtown Da Nang a marine was found with his privates cut off and stuffed in his mouth, an act that sent a clear and unmistakable message. In the history of indigenous warfare on the American plains, cutting off a man's manhood was often a final insult to an enemy.

For the first few months at Da Nang I was satisfied by the work, evenings at the enlisted men's club, and an occasional letter from my mom. Turning twenty years old, however, I was often, to quote my friend Pinkerton, "so hard a cat couldn't have scratched it." We made frequent forays to the ubiquitous skivvy houses that ringed the airbase, frequently catching a dose of the clap. Every morning a long line of marines stood outside the sick bay tent, waiting for venereal shots, one in each ass cheek. One morning an officer who worked in the administration offices lined up with us. Officers may have had their own club at which to drink, but clap treated us all the same.

Downtown Da Nang also lured us. The combat engineers were responsible for unloading much of the war materiel as it came ashore on huge ships from the states. We preferred this duty since the docks were only a few blocks away from the Da Nang commercial center. When paperwork for war equipment wasn't in order and a long wait was anticipated, we would slip away to the bars and skivvy houses. After several successful forays into downtown Da Nang, I threw caution to the winds. Military police, though, caught me coming out of a bar. I was given office hours. Major Campo, our huge commanding officer who flew jet fighters, reprimanded me for being in downtown Da Nang. He wasn't receptive to my explanation – the ship hadn't been ready to be unloaded and I had walked into the heart of Da Nang to have a look-see.

"What I should do is take you outside and kick your ass," the major growled, looking me directly in the eyes.

I stared his challenge back, being young, in good shape, and accustomed to fighting.

Major Campo leaned back into his chair. "No, I think what you need is some good Marine Corps discipline. We're geared to handle people like you."

He sentenced me to thirty days in the Third MAF brig. Due to a rapid growth of incarcerated marines, the brig had just been relocated and wasn't quite completed. It sat by itself on the far side of Hill 327, a few miles from our compound. Every morning the jungle of Vietnam and the cordillera in the distance greeted about four hundred marines locked up there.

My sentence was hard labor. Our first task was to dig a trench around the brig, fifty yards out from its perimeter of barbed and razor wire. The trench added security; marines would be stationed in it as nighttime guards. No machinery was used; four hundred young marines who were guarded by other marines with shotguns and pistols and who relied on picks and shovels dug a trench measuring four feet wide and six feet deep in surprisingly little time.

After digging for a few days, a shout suddenly went up a short distance from where I was working. We could see marines pounding the ground with picks and shovels, killing, we later learned, a ten-foot python. When we went into the brig compound for the noon meal, some of the marines draped the huge snake over their shoulders, carried it to the brig entrance, and laid it along the barbed wire fence.

There is an old belief that a snake doesn't completely die until the sun goes down; it may be true. At the end of the day, we had to wait outside the gate and be checked before reentering the brig compound. This delay was necessary because some marines had been caught smoking dope in the brig, obtaining it from Vietnamese civilians while out on working parties. While we were waiting to be readmitted, the large python, lying all afternoon a few feet away along the barbed wire fence, suddenly drew itself into a ball and then stretched out again.

By the time I served my thirty-day sentence, my tour of Vietnam had concluded. I voluntarily extended my tour of duty, however, for six months: I wanted to be sent back to Vietnam for a second tour, and I liked the Vietnamese people. On one of my days off, I walked far into the jungle by myself – my fellow marines thought I was crazy for doing so – and eventually wandered into a small Vietnamese village. To this day I remember the utter peacefulness of that place. People moved about, doing their chores; in a field a man plowed with a water buffalo; children ran and played. As I stood near a crossroad, debating which direction to go, a man hailed me from a nearby building and offered me a "33," a variety of Vietnamese beer. I sat there and drank beer for a couple of hours and visited with the man. I asked him about Vietnamese life; he inquired about American Indians. He spoke the usual pidgin English, but we understood each other enough to make it interesting and sometimes amusing. He gave me one last beer as a gift and invited me to return and meet his family (they were away in Da Nang). I promised to do so but never did. I really enjoyed that day in Vietnam.

My interactions with the Vietnamese were not limited to that village. At night I had secretly been going out into the village of Hoa Phat, adjacent to our compound and off limits after 6:00 p.m. During the day, because of its proximity to our camp, Hoa Phat bustled with soldiers. Vietnamese beer, Vietnamese girls – the soldier kind – trinkets, souvenirs, Vietnamese handicrafts, and all manner of things could be purchased in the village of Hoa Phat. The marines nicknamed the village Dogpatch, based on the Li'l Abner cartoon strip.

One afternoon when sauntering through the village looking at various items for sale, I ended up on the veranda of a house that sold beer.

When the girl who waited tables there came out of the house, I was stunned by her beauty. Although like many Indians I was shy around girls, she apparently sensed my energy and interest. After serving a couple of other marines and taking my order, she noticed an Indian head tattoo on my left forearm (I had gotten the tattoo while at Camp Pendleton). That interested her; we began talking. Like others at beer-skivvy houses, the girl served marines more than just beer. I drank a few beers and paid the mama san for the girl. It was a hot afternoon; skivvy houses on those kinds of days were far from romantic, with flies buzzing around in the turgid heat. Unlike many of the girls I had bought, this girl was very hirsute and beautiful. When I told her this, she laughed and said her father was a Frenchman. Like me, he had been a foreign soldier who frequented a skivvy house, and she was the result of that desultory lovemaking affair. Other skivvy house girls whom I had patronized were often congenial but businesslike after the fact; this girl sat with me between waiting on tables as I drank a couple of more beers.

When I told her I had to be going, she asked if I could come back at night. "At night I don't work," she said, simply.

I had never been in love before. I think I fell in love that day. Today, when I hear a certain Robbie Robertson song about a lover who won't allow anything to stop him from getting to his paramour, I think of that Vietnamese-French woman and remember that hot day. Her name was Thu Ba.

Truck drivers made it possible for me to slip into Dogpatch and see Thu. While working on the docks in Da Nang, I had made the acquaintance of a number of civilian truck drivers who drove the big trucks for Raymond, Morrison, Knudsen – RMK was a massive civilian conglomerate that apparently made scads of money during the war. The trucks laden with war materiel often passed through our compound before heading on. After dark I would hang around the entrance to the airfield on the U.S. Air Force side, which was still manned by marine military police. When one of the drivers I knew appeared at the gate, I would catch a ride to the other side of the field. On the way I would ask the driver if he would be my accomplice in getting out to Dogpatch, the request usually sweetened by a joint of marijuana or a drink of good American whiskey. A marine riding in the civilian trucks was not an unusual sight, because sometimes we were needed as guides, showing the drivers where to haul their loads, or as protection. It was still a risky proposition. The road through Dogpatch consisted of one long stretch of road to Hill 327, all monitored by military police. If any vehicle stopped, the police would jump immediately into their jeeps and rush into Dogpatch to find out why.

"Yeah, well, you don't have to stop," I'd tell the drivers. "You don't even have to hit your brakes. If your brake lights don't come on, the MPs won't even know you let me off." When a truck would near the end of Hoa Phat village, a half mile from the MP gate, the driver would slow to about ten miles per hour and I would jump into the darkness. In a few minutes I would be at the back door of Thu's house, and she would let me in. She lived with an uncle and an aunt; sometimes, if I had found a ride early in the night, they would still be awake and we would visit with them in the living room.

The pidgin English conversations were not easy but somehow familiar. Many years later, after digesting what had happened to the Native American peoples after the coming of the Europeans, I began to understand my connections to the Vietnamese through their understanding of nature and family, animist beliefs, and Buddhism.

My deception proved successful for about three months, a deception fueled by love for a woman – a very beautiful woman – who made her money serving beer and sleeping with American soldiers. She was another casualty of JFK, Johnson, McNamara, et al.

That love finally got the best of me one morning when I arose too late to get out of the village before dawn. I would normally rise early, walk along the tree line and through the rice paddies until I was a mile or more from the village, and then make my way to the road. By that time the military would have begun its new day of war, so it wasn't difficult to catch a ride in the heavy morning traffic back to the compound; the driver would assume I was coming from one of the military outfits ringing Hill 327. On that fateful morning, I had been working steadily for about a month and had been promised the next day off by the gunnery sergeant. After the military police spotted me and phoned my gunnery sergeant, I learned that I was considered AWOL – apparently my leave had been canceled. I was furious at being caught and at the gunnery sergeant for going back on his word.

The MPs finished their paperwork on me, and I walked over to our company headquarters. Choosing to stay outside, I yelled for the gunnery sergeant to come out.

When he came to the screen door, I cussed him out. "You son of a bitch, you said I had today off!"

"What did you call me?" he asked.

"You're a son of a bitch," I shouted back.

He turned back into the office, and soon the MPs appeared and took me to their headquarters. One of them drove me over to battalion headquarters, where a psychologist questioned me for about half an hour and then released me to the MP, who drove me directly to Major Campo's office.

The Major didn't seem as angry this time. "You've been here going on sixteen months," he announced. "I think you're going native on us. I'm going to give you another thirty days in the brig, and then you're going back to the states. That's all."

The second stint in the Third MAF brig wasn't like the first tour. The prisoners had finished digging the perimeter trench, so our hard labor consisted of knocking down an old cement French fort several miles from the brig. We were ordered to demolish the French fort with sledgehammers and then load the chunks of concrete into the back of a six-by-six near an area called Red Beach. There were numerous military units stationed near Red Beach, and I had gone into the area on several occasions with pieces of heavy equipment to do work for other units. Marines, soldiers, and Seabees frequented the Red Beach area. After we loaded the six-by-six with concrete chunks, we would board, ride a few miles, dump the concrete blocks, and load again. Hard labor.

I did enjoy riding through the verdant and lush Vietnamese countryside in the back of a six-by-six. A marine with a shotgun and a .45-caliber pistol rode guard on us. He was cool; when one of the brig marines lit up a joint of marijuana, the guard – more commonly known as a brig chaser – wouldn't protest. On one hot day I remember riding in the six-by-six with artillery going off in the distance. Skyhawks, F-4B Phantoms, cargo planes, helicopters, and commercial planes soared through the sky, while below, their earthly counterparts roared and whizzed, carrying out the war. And the Vietnamese went about their business. On that hot day, as usual, we were making ourselves as comfortable as we could get on a pile of concrete chunks and taking turns on a joint. A burly, redheaded marine leaned over the cab of the six-by-six and looked ahead. Suddenly, I saw him reach down, grab a large, fifty-pound concrete block, and, without a word, hurl the concrete block over the side of the truck. Sitting on the side of the truck over which he had thrown the block of concrete, I spun and saw an old Vietnamese man tumbling down the side of the built-up roadway, tumbling with his bicycle headfirst into the shallow water of the rice paddy below the road.

"Fuckin' gooks," muttered the redheaded marine, turning back to watch the road ahead. Our big truck rumbled on in the heat.

"You mighta killed that old motherfucker," somebody said.

Never turning around, the marine answered simply, "Hate them motherfuckers."

What I had just witnessed was not war but racial hatred. Many years later, after having joined the American Indian Movement in the early 1970s, that thrown block, that intense hatred, would come back to me, and again the old man would plummet down the steep embankment, his bike tumbling after. How awkward and frail he looked as he hit the water. Did he survive? I eventually realized that what I had seen had in fact taken place over and over as the Europeans stormed into a so-called New World and into the American West. Other old men – my grandfathers – had suffered similar treatment at the hands of American soldiers.

The legacy of that misunderstanding, that hatred, that prejudice, persists. In early 1967, longstanding racial tensions in the cities of America were erupting in race riots. In Vietnam one day that year, it was searingly hot as we stood in line waiting to enter the brig mess hall for chow. Off to our right sixty yards away were the hooches, called hardback tents because they were roofed in tin. The hooches were built about eighteen inches off the ground and consisted of two-by-fours with plywood floors. Twelve men slept in each one. On that day I was standing quite a ways back in the chow line with another Indian, Louis "Butch" Armstrong, who coincidentally also hailed from Cut Bank (I hadn't known Louis was in Vietnam or in the Marine Corps until our paths crossed in the brig).[1]

Several black marines suddenly came out of their hooch and started toward the chow line. Something was wrong; they headed for the front end of the chow line, not wanting to stand in the rear and wait under the pulsing sun. The marines already standing in line saw them coming; when the black marines stepped to the front, they protested. Shoving soon escalated into punches being thrown, and within moments a large melee was taking place.

The fight occurred just a few feet away from the MP gate, and the military police were soon trying to separate the fighters without much success. A helmeted staff sergeant, carrying a shotgun, emerged from the administration building. Aiming over the heads of the combatants, he fired twice, the boom of the shotgun sufficient to cease hostilities, at least for the time being.

"Sit down, motherfuckers, and shut up!"

We all sat down. Nobody argues with a man holding a shotgun.

In a moment the brig commander, a colonel, came out and demanded to know what the hell was going on, castigating us for fighting
among ourselves when – he then gestured toward the distant cordillera
– the true enemy was out there. White men have never understood
how dark-skinned men perceive their true enemy.

The fight in the chow line had strong racial overtones, and that
evening in the hooches we knew something was brewing. After the
guards walked through the area and announced lights out, some of
the white marines who had been in the thick of the brawl were called
out from their hooch for more fisticuffs with the black marines. Verbal
sniping was quickly followed by fighters on both sides piling out of
their hooches. I had retired three hooches down from where the new
brawl was erupting. Why get involved in a rugged battle that was
someone else's fight? The MPS broke up the melee with nightsticks
and flashlights and were backed by others carrying shotguns. The
racial clashes continued into subsequent nights for a week, and the
guards soon found it necessary to shoot over the top of the fighters to
separate and subdue them. The fighting rapidly became more deadly,
as the preferred weapon became the three-foot hardwood sticks that
braced the end of our military cots. By the mornings, marines – black
and white – had received severe wounds. I continued to stay out of
the battle; getting hit in the face with a piece of three-foot hickory
hardwood in the dark of night was not at all appealing.

I didn't fully understand the depth of this hatred between black and
white. I was too young and dumb about racial matters to understand
the fights through a meaningful perspective. I was Indian. I had grown
up in a white border town where there were racial undertones, a few
overtones, but nothing of this violent, overt magnitude. I had run
around with white kids, had dated white girls – though admittedly
their families did not approve – and at camp LeJeune had made friends
with a couple of black guys. Still, I was now twenty-one and the soft
lessons learned in Cut Bank were beginning to jell. The white American doesn't quite seem to realize the great gap he created when he let

his greed get the best of him: with Indians it's treaty rights over the land that was stolen; with blacks it's slavery and its long, drawn-out ramifications. This nocturnal war within a war yielded serious injuries – broken bones, cuts, deep bruises, and at least one cracked skull. But in the Third MAF brig, a place of punishment for men who expected punishment even under ordinary conditions of duty, the wounded returned to the hard labor force after being bandaged and splinted. At least a couple of marines sported casts up to their groins from broken legs received in the riots, probably from being jumped on when they were down.

As the race war in the Third MAF brig intensified, the power of song was soon felt. The clashes began to assume a somewhat formal – and surreal – atmosphere after a few nights, as the blacks began preparing for the nightly fight by singing a kind of African chant. Where the chant originated remains a mystery; it almost seemed made up, sounding like something a non-tribal person would sing in imitation of a tribal song. I have sung on a drum and danced to it; I know the sound of tribal drumming and singing. The chant the blacks sang in the brig sounded like *ooga booga*. It had a real purpose, though, even if it was an impromptu creation. The song forged an identity that reached into the heart of black Africa, letting the white marines know they weren't dealing with slaves. It was black tribalism sprung full-blown in the heat and heart of Vietnam. It connoted spears and painted faces; it was the Heart of Darkness throbbing dangerously in those hot nights. To counter the dark, powerful singing – it would have been laughable had the situation not been so dire – the white marines sang a country western song. I remember the tune as something bizarre, like a Hank Williams song, "Your Cheatin' Heart." Hank Williams versus Idi Amin. Years later, traveling with the American Indian Movement, I would come to understand the power of a song, the cohesive effect of a song for people fighting for a cause.[2]

Decades later, I still sometimes hear those hardwood sticks finding

their marks in the inky Vietnamese night. It was especially dangerous for the white boys in the brig because they didn't have superior
technology, the one thing that had allowed them to transport black
people from Africa and wrest control of homelands away from American Indians. Everyone had to fight with clubs, and the white marines
suffered. Eventually the brig commander posted an all-night guard
with a riot gun to walk the hooches after dark. The nightly riots soon
ended.[3]

One evening in the brig we huddled in trenches dug behind our
hooches as Russian-made rockets screamed and sped overhead, ex-
ploding on the Da Nang airfield where hundreds of aircraft were
parked. The rockets sounded like giant, ungainly birds as they flew
overhead in the night. As we had scrambled to get in the trenches, one
white marine who had received a broken ankle during the race riots
slipped and fell into the trench, breaking his wrist.

In a few minutes a gunship appeared. This type of gunship, nicknamed Puff the Magic Dragon, was a modified transport plane outfit-
ted with Gatling guns that could fire six thousand rounds a minute.
Locating the supposed point where the rockets had been fired, a steady
stream of red – tracer bullets – spewed from the plane to the ground.
The guns fired so rapidly it created the illusion of a red piece of thread
hanging from the plane to the earth. The Gatling guns sounded like a
piece of cloth tearing, not the staccato sound of an M-60 machine gun
but a continuous roar, truly a dragon sound. Soon a helicopter gunship appeared and began firing cannons into the suspected Viet Cong
stronghold. As thousands of bullets, backed up by cannon fire, raked
the ground, I began to more clearly comprehend what my people had
faced in the American West when the whites came with the Gatling
guns.

Eventually I was released from the brig. The military police escorted
me to my hooch, and I packed my sea bag. The driver of the MP jeep
drove me across the swamp to our work area, where I bid farewell to

my fellow marines and then left for the states. Within minutes I was sitting in a large hangar with hundreds of other marines waiting for a plane to take us back to the world.

I never saw Thu Ba again. It's been over thirty years since I saw that beautiful face, but sometimes I think of her.

What was the legacy of Vietnam for me? I liked and felt a bond with the Vietnamese people. Listening to the white soldiers castigate them for their supposedly uncivilized lifestyle taught me a lesson that wouldn't fully be appreciated until I took part in the Wounded Knee standoff in 1973. As white soldiers, federal marshals, FBI agents, state troopers, and the 182nd Airborne hunted and shot at me and other Indians during the siege, the entire Vietnamese scenario began to flesh itself out, taking shape slowly, focusing through the haze that was created in Cut Bank and in marine boot camp. Vietnam became a wide screen upon which the issues of race and oppression flashed in an increasingly brighter luminescence as the tracer bullets sang menacingly over my head in the bunker at Wounded Knee. The image of that old Vietnamese man rolling down the rice paddy dike came back to me, and the connections became clear and ominous and deadly. I was living in a country whose people would use me for their own reasons and then turn their guns on me when I no longer suited their purpose.

Returning

6

It is 1967. When we arrive at Fatima base in Okinawa, we are processed to return to the states, a lengthy and bureaucratic procedure of wait and more wait. We are checked for contraband (weapons, ammo, etc.). A marine standing near me carries a miracle helmet. It's his combat helmet, complete with a hole where a bullet had entered, zinged around inside, and yet never harmed him. His company commander had written a note authorizing him to take the helmet home.

We were supposed to stay on base and wear our military fatigues until we reached the states. I did neither. I made friends with a marine who had been stationed at Okinawa before being sent to Vietnam and who had acquaintances on the base. (We had been authorized to go to the enlisted men's club during processing; alcohol was served there, including hard liquor that had been hard to get in Vietnam.) My friend's acquaintances got us some civilian clothes for a few dollars, and we snuck off the base by hiding in the trunk of an Okinawan taxicab. Soon we were wilding in the raucous bars of the village of Fatima, drinking and whoring. I remember waking up alone in a hotel room, the sun high, and my money supply low. The good-looking Okinawan bargirl I had paid to sleep with was gone, and I didn't know where my friend was. We later ran into each other and spent another night out in the town of Fatima. Returning to the base the following day – due more to a lack of money than party fatigue – we discovered that our unit had already departed for the states. Following a good harangue by the sergeant in charge of departures, we were put on the next flight. The sun was just coming up and I was hung over as we lifted off. Sleeping the sleep of the truly alcohol-fatigued, I finally woke up when we had left daylight behind and were flying through darkness, a darkness that took us down the west coast of the United States and to Norton Air Base. It was good to touch down and to know we were back in our home country. Some of us had a couple of drinks at a lounge in the terminal. Everyone was anxious to return home, however, and soon we went our separate ways – hailing cabs, catching buses, going to other airports, and finally going home. We had become veterans of a foreign war.

I didn't return home immediately, not having saved much money while in Vietnam. I bought a bus ticket to San Francisco and visited my nephew, John Hirst Jr., who was attending a diesel mechanic school there. John and I practically had been raised together, since he was only about fifteen months younger than I. John was as impoverished as I was – living as a student on a BIA stipend didn't allow for much spending cash. There was, however, money available for me: I had funds in the BIA office on the Blackfeet reservation, since I had inherited several hundred acres of trust land from my biological mother, Lucille Monroe. The morning that I wired for the money, neither John nor I could afford the bus fare to the Western Union office; that evening I was twenty-five hundred dollars richer. We partied hearty for a couple of days, and then I bought us both plane tickets home. John arranged to take his spring exams a little early so he could come home with me.

I never saw John alive again. A few days after my leave expired, I reported late to Camp Pendleton, California, and as punishment was assigned to mess duty for a month. After finishing mess duty, I was told to re-qualify at the rifle range, an annual requirement for marines. One day at the rifle range I was lying down, dry firing, when a man in civilian clothes walked up and introduced himself as a Red Cross representative. He said that my nephew, John Hirst Jr., while working as a representative for an insurance firm in Ohio, had fallen into a pool during a party and drowned. John could be rather testy when drinking – whether he actually fell into the pool due to inebriation or had been fighting at the pool's edge and was knocked into the water, we never learned. He would be the first of four brothers to die violent deaths, three of them before the age of thirty. Years later, in the mid-1970s, John appeared to me in a dream and told me never to fear dying. In the dream I was in a hospital room looking at him in a hospital bed (knowing in my mind that he was dead, the way one can read things in dreams without anything being said). Suddenly he sat up, smiling, and said, "Don't ever be afraid to die."

My time at Camp Pendleton first brought me into contact with the counterculture. Growing up Catholic in cattle country and serving in the marines had cemented some very strong conservative ideas in my mind. But Scott Mckenzie was singing about going to San Francisco and wearing flowers in his hair that summer of '67. Although I did not join the hippies who were heading for San Francisco that Summer of Love, the concepts of nonviolence and abhorrence to war began to take root within my consciousness. Although my relationship with hippies would be shattered a half decade later in a violent brawl in the Wine Shacks of Missoula, their message that summer never let go. I was beginning to understand that what I had seen and experienced in Vietnam was an atrocity against the human spirit.

I was still a private when I reached Camp Pendleton. I had lost my Private First Class ranking when I was thrown in the brig in Vietnam and had been passed over for promotion since. It didn't really bother me. I took the GED test and received the highest score in the battalion. Captain Cook, the company commander, announced the accolade just before PT one morning. I was as surprised as some of the other marines in my unit – Indians weren't supposed to get higher scores than white guys on academic tests.

Indians seek each other out, and soon I had a Pueblo friend and a Navajo friend, Eugene Louis (who racked with me – I slept on the lower bunk), both drinkers and partiers. We would go to the little seaside town of Oceanside where I would drink my meager pay. Marines are supposed to drink, fight, and fuck. I did quite a lot of the first two – I once fought a sergeant in a bar called the Copper Door and still have a scar on the base of my left thumb where his teeth were locked like a bulldog's. Available women, however, were quite scarce in Oceanside; thousands of marines on the base meant only a few barmaids to choose from for dates.

One night in Oceanside I did manage to meet a very good-looking woman in a bar, the wife of somebody on base. Earlier that day my Navajo friend, Eugene Louis, and I had picked up some western-style belts we had ordered in town. (A couple of weeks earlier we had ridden in a base rodeo and met a marine who was both a rodeo cowboy and worked for a leather shop in town.) The belts were personalized with our names in black letters on the back. After Louis returned to base, I went around the bars with my new belt in a sack. The good-looking wife owned a nice car, a Thunderbird, and after the bars closed we drove around a bit. She wasn't interested in having sex and just wanted someone to talk to about her problems. When she dropped me off at the bus depot, I forgot my personalized belt in her glove compartment. I hoped she would find the belt before her husband did. For days afterward I would jump whenever ordered to the administrative offices; I pictured an irate husband standing there with my new belt in one hand and a pistol in the other.

My Navajo friend did get shot. At a country and western bar one night, Louis met an older white woman whose husband was in Vietnam. She took him home. A few nights later, his testosterone having built to a throbbing level again, he returned to the country and western bar. He stayed until closing time, drinking and waiting for her.

Unsuccessful, Louis decided to walk to her house. The topography that night was not at all in focus for my friend as he stumbled up to and knocked boldly on what he thought was the older woman's door. Someone inside yelled for him to go away. But Louis became insistent, pleading with the woman to let him in, let him in the house, let him in her. A shot rang out and Louis – immediately sober – dashed off the porch and at terrific Navajo speed sped toward the bus station a half mile away. Returning from Oceanside later that evening (I really didn't care for country and western music, though it's listened to the most on reservations), I learned that Louis had been shot in the stomach and was at the base hospital. Undressing for bed later, I noticed Louis's T-shirt on his rack. The lights were out in the squad bay, but from the streetlight filtering through the window, I could see blood on the T-shirt and two holes, one in front and one in back. A .22 bullet had gone clean through him, luckily without hitting any crucial organs. Louis spent a few days in the hospital and was soon back at work, subjected to ribbing by the other marines. We never knew whether he had even found the right house.

My Indian friends and I also traveled frequently on the bus to Los Angeles, looking for more Indians. We found them in the seedy area known as Third and Main. It was skid row. On weekends, Indians from tribes all over the country frequented places like the Ritz Bar, Gus's Bar, the Columbine, the Moulin Rouge, and the Irish Pub. Indians drank, fought, committed adultery, and socialized as best they could in an urban setting.

Fights were always taking place in and around the Indian bars. Sometimes it was intertribal – Navajos against Sioux, Kiowas against Comanches – more often it was individuals quarreling because their spouses, girlfriends, or boyfriends were becoming too friendly with someone else. One time, Louis and I had just bought something to eat at a little eatery called Johnny's Shrimp Boat across from the Ritz. In the parking lot behind the place we came across a fight between two Indians, both big, thick waisted, and swinging for the head. A woman called out to Tiger, one of the fighters. Ultimately, Tiger went down under a savage, bare-knuckled assault and was given the boot.

On another Saturday night, after spending most of our money, Louis and I each bought a pint of whiskey and walked the streets, stopping in an alley now and then to take a pull from our flasks. Passing the door of the Columbine, which was run by an ex-professional wrestler and from which poured splashy country music, we decided to wait outside and hustle women as they arrived and left the bar. We wanted women, women without any men with them. We didn't have any luck until closing time, when the bar disgorged a crowd of Mexicans, poor whites, some blacks, and Indians full of booze and whiny country music. We spotted three women walking together, two visibly Indian and one with fair skin and reddish hair. We were forward, whiskey-brave forward. The women, finding out we had liquor, invited us to join them at the Tombs.

In 1968, after the bars closed, the LA Indians would retire to the Tombs, a place of ghostly, massive pillars under one of myriad freeways. There was always a big crowd at the Tombs on Saturday night, singing, fighting, and loving. Indians have a way of finding some place to gather after hours to continue the partying. When they get some alcohol under their belt, the suppressed Indian culture starts coming out. Probably the most obvious way is singing tribal songs, a distinct identity that clarifies those gray areas they live in as they go about their jobs, schooling, or hoboing.

My friend Floyd told me a story of love from the Tombs. He was in a parked car with a beautiful girl from the Southwest who asked him to hold her tight. His arms already around her, Floyd gave a tighter, vise-grip squeeze. Immediately she started gasping for breathe and bent over in pain. He had squeezed too hard and had cracked two of her ribs.

As I've said, Indians are a violent people on liquor. You'd see a big crowd of Indians gathered around someone's car, pounding on the hood, singing forty-nine songs and five minutes later, the whole damn crew would be rolling on the ground fighting. People would get beat up, yet the following weekend they'd be back pounding on the car hood. When drunk, Indians act out plot lines and scripts written by others. Since Europeans usurped the Native homelands, the stories and images many Indian men grew up with, the values they learn, are largely the products of white culture – toughness and violence. They don't stop to consider the earlier times of great peacefulness, when the camps were content and full of meat, and the lodges were warm and comforting. Indians are by nature a gregarious people, always ready for a celebration. As white men swept west, some would complain about the Indians constantly feasting, dancing, and making light of the great problem that was life, always pouring themselves into the inveterate crucible of merrymaking as if it really mattered. That merrymaking took on a different hue with the introduction of alcohol, took on a deadly intonation our grandfathers and grandmothers didn't have to worry about after an evening of lightness and laughter.

It was on one of these weekend drinking trips – again with Louis – to Los Angeles that I met the woman who would become my wife for nearly eighteen years. I was twenty-two years old when Zelda Jean Harwood, thirty-five years old, came into my life one February night. Jean's great-grandfather had come to Montana on the Texas cattle drives and had married Little Antelope Woman, a Blackfoot. Jean is redheaded, and to see her on the street you would think her a white woman, but she grew up around Indians and knew things like playing stick game. She would play Indian music on her eight-track tape deck, the first time I had ever heard Indian music in a hi-tech format. Jean was attending nursing school in the LA area. She had twice been married when we met and had three daughters by each marriage – Desiree, Consuella, Gloria, Patricia, Teresa, and Lita. Her oldest daughter was fourteen; the youngest, seven.

It certainly wasn't the conventional boy meets girl story. I fell in love with a redheaded Indian woman who had six children. Maybe it was simply a part of the craziness that was going on all over the country in 1968: the Summer of Love had just ended; Bobby Kennedy and Martin Luther King Jr. were assassinated; Lyndon Johnson was refusing the nomination to the U.S. presidency; Woodstock loomed a year away, followed shortly by the Indian occupation of Alcatraz. To this day I am not sure of the real basis of our attraction – I was closer in age to the oldest daughter than to the mother – but it happened, rapidly. Soon I was making my way to Los Angeles every weekend to see her, and on weekends when I couldn't get leave, she would visit Camp Pendleton.

In the late summer of 1968, Jean's nurse training ended and she decided to move back home to Montana with her children. We didn't actually promise to meet in Montana, but I told her I would be getting out of the corps shortly – in September – and I also planned on going home.

On the Saturday afternoon before she left, Jean drove to Camp Pendleton with a couple of friends, Indian women, and picked me up. Her cousin Dick Harwood, who was also stationed at the base, joined us. Dick, like other members of the Harwood family (in fact, like many half-blood families) had been brought up in the cowboy culture – rodeo was his thing. In my future wife's old Cadillac, a '57 model with fins jutting skyward, we sped down the coast that afternoon to the little inland town of Escondido, where we were soon ensconced in a bar called the Silver Dollar. After an hour or so of drinking, we decided to move on. As we left, Dick spotted a western wear store that featured a plastic statue of a steer as part of its advertising. The steer was nearly life-size, four feet tall at the shoulder. Dick, coming from a rodeo family and with just enough beer in him to bring out that rough cowboy sense of humor, walked over to the steer and pretended to put a steer wrestling hold on it. He gave a twist, but instead of going down, the steer's head broke off. We laughed at this not-so-stout steer's fate and then roared off to find another bar. Someone must have witnessed the steer debacle, wrote our license plate down, and notified the police of the vandalism.

We decided we needed gas before we launched into another round of drinking. After gassing the caddy, Dick – he'd had a couple of shots of whiskey along with the beer at the Silver Dollar – pulled toward the street but missed the driveway. He drove the old Cadillac off the sidewalk, the big car's rear wheels came off the ground, and we became hopelessly high-centered. What a spectacle – only drunks in their dimwitted fog of alcohol can get into such precarious and utterly ridiculous situations. With cars whizzing by and drivers craning their heads, we lined up on the front and tried pushing the car rearward. That, of course, didn't work.

We were at a bit of a loss when a police cruiser arrived. A big, beefy officer slowly walked around to the back of the caddy, looked at the license plate, and then told Dick he was under arrest for malicious mischief. But we had more problems. Given the odd angle of the car, Dick was asked to undergo a sobriety test by walking a straight line. He failed the test; his cowboy boots with high-tapered riding heels would have made it difficult to walk a straight line even if the Pope had worn them.

Our weekend was being ruined. I protested, using some marine talk on the cop. My interference resulted in being handcuffed and put in the squad car with Dick.

And the situation became even worse. They thought we were Mexicans. Escondido, apparently, did not have its own jail, or they didn't want us there. We were taken to the San Diego County jail along with two Indians – big Indians, fat Indians, drunken Indians who had been fighting each other and were still cussing each other out as they were being loaded into our cruiser. Dick, the most light-skinned of us, was put in the front seat with the cop. I sat in back between the two combatants, handcuffed to them both. I tried to be congenial with my fellow prisoner-passengers, asking about their tribe (always the first question an Indian asks another Indian). My attempt at good manners became moot when the Indian on my right suddenly remembered something from the earlier fight and decided to retaliate. Swinging his free arm across me to the face of the Indian on my left, his blow sent the other Indian's face smashing against the window. The response was equally swift; the Indian on my left swung with his free left hand, and I was caught handcuffed in the middle of a one-handed boxing scuffle, catching blows that weren't intended for me. I began shouting for the cop to do something, and he finally pulled over and the Indians quit fighting. One of the men was moved to the front seat and Dick joined me in back. We spent the night in jail and went to court. Because Dick and I were marines, we were released and fined; Dick's fine was much greater because of the steer head and being under the influence at the wheel.

Dick had a little over three years left to live. The cowboy marine who had wrestled a head off a plastic steer would one night, at ninety miles an hour, drive under the rear end of a semi outside of Billings, decapitating himself. I would be a pallbearer.

My time in the military was drawing to a close. I was a short-timer, which meant being assigned all manner of trivial duties just before getting out. With about a month remaining, I was ordered (ironically) to oversee the work details of brig prisoners. Each day I would collect about a dozen prisoners at the brig and shepherd them through the day as they, carrying a duffel bag and a stick with a nail in the end, picked up trash from the roadways.

One day we were picking debris along a roadway in Area 26 of Camp Pendleton when one of the prisoners called out to me. He had found a full bottle of Thunderbird wine that someone had ditched; alcohol wasn't allowed on base except for at the service clubs. I told him to put it in his bag. At the end of the day, as the prisoners sat at a small tool shed waiting for the bus from the brig to pick them up, they cajoled me into letting them drink the wine. I stood watch while they drank from the wine bottle. It was a hot day. Among the prisoners was John Murray, a Blackfoot marine from back home. John took a couple of horrendous drinks. In about ten minutes the wine hit him, and soon he was talking a mile a minute, his tongue loosened by the alcohol. By the time we returned to the brig, John was feeling pretty good, talking animatedly, and I was sure the prison personnel would become suspicious.[1]

A week previous to the wine drinking, I had lost a prisoner in the mess hall. He had leaped over the food line and ran out the back door. I couldn't chase him, as I had the other prisoners to watch. When I returned to the brig with my charges, the brig duty officer called me in and told me that in the past they had made the brig chaser serve the time of the prisoner until the prisoner was recaptured. My heart sank. I had no desire to go back into the brig; my two stints in Vietnam were plenty. Luckily, they let me go after writing out in detail the circumstances of the escape and a map showing the route and method of escape.

I was discharged from the Marine Corps on September 13, 1968.

Awakening 7

My trail now led back to a changing world. In late 1968 my father had been dead for three years. My mother still lived in Cut Bank, now alone. Big John continued to run the family ranch and a few years earlier had adopted a twenty-two month old boy, Martin James Still Smoking.[1] Max lived in Spokane, Washington, as did Katherine, and they both had children. Aurise was working on a cattle ranch as a cook. Quentin had been dead for ten years.

I too was changing, albeit slowly. I was becoming aware of an America that was being determined by the color of my skin. The Woody Kipp discharged from the Marine Corps in 1968 was becoming increasingly different than the Woody Kipp who had left Cut Bank four years earlier. Whatever potion was inciting the anti-Vietnam protests, the civil rights marches, and the sexual revolution was also working on me. Lessons learned on the Blackfeet reservation, in the border town of Cut Bank, in North Carolina, in Vietnam, and later in California were beginning to crystallize. I began to understand why they couldn't give me the award for the essay in junior high school; I was not an American, in the mainstream sense of the word. I was coming to see Nigger Jim differently than the white boys I had served with in Vietnam. The connotations of Joseph Conrad's *Heart of Darkness* increasingly became easier to grasp as the years rolled forward. Kurtz had jailed me. I had lived with Kurtz, fought for Kurtz, trusted Kurtz, and now

I didn't. The Viet Cong dethroned Kurtz. Kurtz was powerful, but he wasn't invincible. He had some weak spots. That was good to know.

During my first few days out of the Marine Corps, I partied in the LA Indian bars and soon ran out of money. After a wild weekend of partying, one of my women friends, who was dating Jean's cousin Dick, encouraged me to stay in the city with them until Dick received his discharge from the Marine Corps in three weeks. Dick's girlfriend lived with her sister, a Blackfeet and a medical secretary in a Hollywood doctor's office, and her sister's boyfriend, Larry, an Indian from the Southwest. Larry got me a job with him at the Atherton Roofing Company, replacing a Mexican who had quit. My job was to keep the tar pot boiling for the roofers.

I thus spent the remainder of 1968 in Los Angeles, working for the Atherton Roofing Company all week and partying on the weekends. I was far from home but discovered that other Blackfeet were living in the city; some had moved through the relocation program initiated by the BIA some years before, and a few attended college.

My personal and work situation in Los Angeles continued to change; through no design of my own, I soon had Larry's job and girlfriend. On one Wednesday evening, three days after I began work, Larry, his girlfriend, Dick's girlfriend, and I were eating dinner in their small apartment, when we heard a knock at the door. Two very tall and officious looking white men in suits entered the room, and in three minutes had apprehended Larry and left with him. Larry was AWOL from the Marine Corps, and not for the first time. His girlfriend had experienced this once before, when Larry had served six months in the brig.

At work the next morning I reported to the owner of the roofing company what had happened to his roofer. Shaking his head, he told me to work as a roofer until more help could be hired. On the Friday following the arrest, I came home from work to discover that Dick's girlfriend had given up waiting for Dick and was returning to Montana. I found out later that Dick had been reluctant to drive back home with his LA girlfriend because he had a fiancée on the reservation. With everyone out of the picture, Larry's ex-girlfriend and I began an affair. For the next three months until I returned to Montana, I filled in for the incarcerated marine boyfriend. Larry had helped me out, but I justified my behavior at the time by reasoning what the hell, she's one of my women, from my tribe. As if I owned the women of my tribe. I still feel a pang of guilt about that whole matter.

My new girlfriend was a bit conservative sexually and was not comfortable being seen unclothed; she would get in bed with her nightgown on. Our lovemaking had been enjoyable but somewhat mechanical. That changed dramatically one morning after Dick's former girlfriend returned from Montana—Dick had returned to his fiancée. We all lived together, and my girlfriend and I slept on a foldout couch in the living room. One morning I woke early and made love to the woman. For whatever reason, she absolutely exploded, her orgasm coming long, loud, and impetuously. I had learned how to make a woman cum.

Prior to that instructive morning, I had been somewhat like a friend of mine in Wisconsin, who apparently has a fairly small penis. He tells a story of getting undressed and the woman he was with, sizing up his equipment, asked him sardonically, "Who do you think you're gonna please with that thing?" He looked her dead in the eye and said, "Me."

Our relationship ended in mid-December when I became enamored of another woman from one of the Indian bars. My girlfriend was jealous. When I went to her apartment to get my clothes, she had already taken a new lover, whom she had picked up the previous weekend at the Moulin Rouge.

I left for Montana, for the Blackfeet reservation, on a Greyhound bus a couple of days after New Year's Day. Unlike those who want to get somewhere as quickly as possible, I have always enjoyed seeing the country; the view from thirty thousand feet in a plane is certainly exhilarating, but I like riding close to the land.

I would never return to the throbbing city of Los Angeles. I had gained some valuable work experience. I also took home with me a growing addiction to alcohol. I was an alcoholic, not alcoholic in the sense of being incapacitated but in frequency of use. What I wasn't able to see at that time—what alcoholics aren't able to comprehend while they're on their downward spiral—was that all of my major problems in life up to that point had been caused by alcohol.[2] I, along with several other basketball players, had been kicked off the basketball team when I was a junior in high school for drinking. We were reinstated, but alcohol was at the root of the banishment. While drunk, I had been beaten severely by black men in Jacksonville, North Carolina; I had my nose broken by a white man in a cheap bar in Great Falls, Montana; and because of my alcohol abuse, I had spent time in the Third MAF brig. Along with these major events in my life, I could add a host of other less debilitating, but nonetheless alcohol-related, events.

It was January 1969, and it was very cold. By the time our bus reached southern Idaho, the temperature had dropped to below zero, and it continued to fall as we headed farther north. When the bus stopped at a small Idaho town, I was dressed thinly and foolishly in a light nylon jacket and jeans, California style. We had a half hour in the small town before resuming. Everybody went into the bus stop cafe; I wasn't hungry and instead braved the sledgehammer effect of really cold air to walk to a bar about a block away, its neon signs clanging against the sub-zero chill. I was the only customer and soon began telling stories of Vietnam to the barmaid.

I told one story too many.

Peering outside at the bus station, the barmaid suddenly exclaimed, "Is that your bus leaving?" Dashing to the door, I saw my bus already moving down the avenue. Running hard in pursuit in the cold night proved futile, and the bus turned onto the freeway ramp, carrying away my discharge papers, clothes, and remaining money.

I became frantic. The manager of the bus station, a small-town white man—who had more pressing things on his mind than an Indian who had missed his bus—shrugged his thin shoulders and, pointing to a hotel down the street, said I could catch a bus tomorrow. But I didn't have money for a room. Suddenly—Jung calls this synchronicity, others call it the Good Lord watching over them—a taxicab appeared at the corner of the bus depot. I dove into the backseat just as it was pulling onto the main street. The driver, an ancient man who listened to my dilemma patiently, turned onto the freeway in pursuit. He was moving too slow, though, on the snow-packed road; the taillights of the bus ahead diminished as it gathered speed. I was up over the back seat urging the driver on, the way a sled dog racer must urge his dogs to greater speed. I then suggested that he blink his lights at the bus. That worked. I was so happy to catch the bus that I gave the old cab driver all the money I had in my wallet, a twenty-dollar bill.

The temperature continued to drop as I neared home, plummeting to more than forty degrees below zero amidst the winds of the high plains. By the time we left Butte and headed toward Helena and then to Great Falls, the air inside the bus was so cold that everybody's breath was visible; the grease on the steering sections of the bus became so congealed that the bus driver had difficulty making turns. In Butte an elderly Blackfoot woman, Cecilia Schildt, who knew my mother, boarded the bus. She sat across from me and visited, telling stories from her early life on the reservation.

The bus coldly and finally arrived in Cut Bank. I was back where I had started from and was glad to see my mom.

I hung around Cut Bank for a few days, looked up a couple of high school friends, and partied a bit; without a job or income, though, it was hard to party in a white town. I thus went to Big John's ranch and started working for my brother, feeding cattle, doctoring calves, fencing, and breaking horses. Big John and Bobby's adopted son, Martin, was about ten years old; Bobby's children from a former marriage were grown and gone.

The winter of 1969 bore down. The Lakotas have a name for that kind of cold—The Moon of the Popping Trees—a cold so intense it bursts the trees. There's not a whole lot to do on a ranch in that kind of weather except keep the stock alive, which included two hundred cattle and forty horses.

Though ranch life was an appealing change, I was twenty-three and wanted companionship. I contacted Jean Harwood who, as I have mentioned, had already returned to Montana from Los Angeles with her family. My redheaded girlfriend came to Big John's ranch. We went to Cut Bank, I introduced her to my mom and found out our families were longtime acquaintances. Jean's aunt, Isabelle, had actually been named for my mom. Her family lived, for the most part, on the southeastern boundary of the Blackfeet reservation. We saw each other fairly frequently after I returned, and in March she was with child.

Spring gradually began to make faint showings. When the landscape has been locked in deep-freeze temperatures and then one day the water trickles down the ruts in the roadways from melting snowbanks, there is a celebratory feeling. It is survival.

The return to my home and my mother was also the beginning of a good-bye. My mom, seventy-five years old, enjoyed exceptional health throughout my lifetime. She had never been in a hospital except to bring one of her grandchildren or me to the emergency room. Mom prayed a lot, not noisily but intensely. She had endured the missionary school travails of most young Indian girls of her generation. I was too young to be aware of the rampant abuses fostered in the missionary system and as such never had the chance to query her or my pop about their experiences with the purported people of God who were given the job of forming young and innocent Indian minds.

My mom passed away in November 1969. She had told people that she prayed that God would allow her to see her children grow and be able to take care of themselves before she passed on. My return from Vietnam (and with a steady girlfriend) seemed to answer her prayer. She had a stroke, lay in the Cut Bank hospital for a couple of weeks in a comatose state, and then was gone.

She was exceptionally kind.

Breaking

8

Like many other Vietnam veterans, no ceremony welcomed me home. My folks, having been schooled by missionaries, did not attend the few ceremonies practiced by the Blackfeet at that time. I had no formal spiritual ceremonial, no easy way to reenter my home community and reconcile my actions overseas. I did adjust, but it took breaking a certain fiery black horse to bring me back fully to the Blackfeet reservation and to the world of my family.

Two great Blackfoot loves – good-looking horses and good-looking women. Cowboys tell a story of an old cowpuncher who was asked on his deathbed what he wanted done with his body. He said, "Well, boys, I want you to take my body and skin it. Use the skin to cover a lady's saddle. That way I'll always be right between the two things in life I love the most." Blackfeet men can relate to that tale. Two things in life of great beauty and power, which are familiar but require much care and meticulous handling if one is to get on with them. I have had better luck with horses.

We no longer run buffalo. We have remained horsemen, but the attitudes that the old people had toward horses, the spiritual attitudes, have been replaced by the attitudes of white cowboys. We treat horses roughly. We cuss when they don't do what we want. We have changed. We haven't changed for the better, but we don't know this yet. We, tribally, were all horse whisperers at one time, communicating with the horse, riding without hands at full tilt so we could shoot the short, heavy bows at the buffalo. The white people assimilated that way out of us. Now we do things roughly, like the white men.

Riding tough horses became a certain kind of high calling for us. When you walk in the Legion Club in Browning, they'll buy you a drink if you're a bronc rider. Many rode the wild horses from the prairies at the Fourth of July Rodeo in Browning. Dan Connolly, who is now in his late eighties and who rode a lot of wild horses in his day, says that for the rodeo they would gather the horses from a wide terrain – the owners didn't matter – and run them into the bucking corrals at the old rodeo grounds west of Browning. When the rodeo was over, they would herd the horses through Browning's main street to the east edge of town and turn them loose. There were no fences, and the horses would start back to their home ranges.

In 1968 about forty head of horses comprised Big John's herd. In the buffalo culture days, horses were the yardstick for measuring wealth, along with the number of wives a man could support. Even in the early reservation years there were thousands of horses roaming the ranges. A few Indians still hold to that particular wreath of satisfaction, keeping horses beyond what they can use. A field of horses is impressive, to say nothing of the beauty they bring to the land, especially the herds that have horses of many colors.

Big John hadn't sold any colts in the years since I had left for the military and now owned quite a few unbroken colts along with some older horses that weren't completely broken. Before I left for the Marine Corps, I had enjoyed fooling around with young, unbroken horses. Though Big John grew up using horses, he never became obsessed with the cowboy image the way so many of us did – big hat, boots, cowboy talk. Eagle Shoe had allowed me to ride the prairies with him on a sorrel mare when I was ten. A bay colt of that mare had been a yearling when I entered the Marine Corps. I remember the colt as long, lean, and extremely wild, a dark bay.

Big John's horse herd was not to be seen around the ranch when I returned in the bitter cold of early 1969. They were out north, maybe down toward Powell Coulee, which was five or six miles away. That part of the country was still in its natural state – shortgrass prairie and buffalo grass. A little farther north toward the Canadian border, white farmers were breaking the sod and moving toward us, acre by acre.

"We should go run those horses in," I suggested to Big John.

He agreed, and we went to find them on his snowmobiles. I rode on a double-track Polaris; he, an Arctic Cat. The horses were gathered right where Big John said they would be, just a little west of Powell Coulee, pawing the knee-deep snow on the flats to find grass. After circling at a distance, we started toward them. When we were a quarter mile away, they began running west and were soon in full flight, the roaring growl of snowmobile engines goading them into fright and flight, their legs sinking into the snow to the knees, the slower, older, heavier horses making a desperate effort to keep up with the younger, fleeter runners.

We kept them at a lope all the way to the home corrals. Forty clouds of steam rose in the still, brittle air of the Montana winter as the horses milled in the corrals. (Three sides of the slab corral were constructed from rough twelve-foot slabs, which were bought from a lumbering operation in Kalispell and were hauled a hundred miles home on the stock truck. It's good protection for heifers during the calving season: the wind can roar at eighty miles per hour, and newly born calves would last only a few minutes in that kind of wind chill. The slab corral is about seventy-five feet across and opens into other corrals, pens, and loading chutes.) We caught a couple of the saddle horses and turned the rest out, throwing them some bales of hay to induce their return. That decision, however, would ultimately hinge on the lead mare's sense of captivity and freedom. Most animals, including humans, can be lured to do one thing or another through their stomachs. But there are horses that were born in the hills and to whom no amount of rich food is sufficient temptation; they'll choose the freedom of the hills, where they will be forced to paw for grass in deep snow, over the safety and dependability of a corral. Freedom comes at a high price.

The lean bay colt that I remembered fondly had similarly proven to be too independent, too free, to join the horses milling in the corral that day. Big John had kept him till he was a three-year-old stud, hoping to make a saddle horse of him and possibly a breeding stallion. The young bay stud, however, had been born in the hills. When they had corralled and roped him as a two-year-old, the bay escaped by going over a seven-foot corral. Horses cannot normally jump seven feet high, but when they're frightened, many will attempt a seven-foot corral pole and be able to get at least their front feet over. With enough momentum, they sometimes will break the top pole, maybe the next pole as well, and flop over to the ground outside the corral, usually dropping in a sideways heap. Gaining their feet, they then stampede away. Sometimes a horse will break its neck in the jump or resulting fall.

After feeding the cattle one morning – Big John driving the pickup while I cut the twine on the bales of hay and portioned them off the back – he asked me to take the big stock truck and go pick up a horse, which was given to him while drinking at the Hi-Mac Tavern in Cut Bank. Gary Pendergrass, a half-blood Blackfeet who owned a ranch west of Cut Bank, had given him the horse, which was supposedly broke to ride. The horse was four years old, tall, lean, and all black except for a left white fetlock, a thoroughbred-quarter-horse cross with more thoroughbred showing in his build. He was greyhound sleek, big chested, wasp waisted, alert, and spooky. Though Pendergrass claimed the horse was broken, he acted awfully snorty when I loaded him into the stock truck.

Back at Big John's Ranch, I put the black horse in the corral where there was feed and water. The next morning, after we fed the cows, Big John drove to the corrals to look over his gift horse. The horse looked "geared pretty high," a favorite saying of an old cowboy I had worked with for the Consolidated Cattle Company, which was on the north end of the Blackfeet reservation, when I was in my teens.

"Gary said they rode him," Big John said, as we looked the horse over. "You wanna try him?"

Did I want to try the black horse? Bravery was a Blackfeet ideal from the old days, an ideal now wrapped in toughness that persisted to the present. I've seen Blackfeet men get in arguments in bars and take up the challenge to fight when there was no way in hell they were going to win, simply because they had that bravery ideal implanted in them at a young age. The coming of the white cowboy and his culture of toughness had only added fuel to an already hot fire.

So, do I want to try the sleek, spooky black horse? The forty-below weather doesn't leave much bounce in the ground; it's hard as pavement. But yeah, I'll try the horse; I'm Blackfeet, ain't I? Fucking right – I'll try the horse, saddle him up, let me get my spurs on, cinch him tight, I don't want my saddle turning. Big John can cinch a horse tight. One time in the mountains after killing some elk, he cinched a horse so tight it lay down.

The black horse stands alone and watches us from the far side of the slab corral. The horse won't be caught in the big slab corral, so we run him into one of the smaller catch pens. After he pivots away a few times, I lay the halter and lead rope on the lodgepole pine corral rails and go after a catch rope. It's been a while since I've roped, but it's like riding a bike – you don't really forget – and after a couple of missed loops, I get the range back and catch him around the neck, jerking the slack until the loop is tight around his throatlatch. He blows air through his nose that comes out in loud, steaming snorts. He's what the cowboys call snaky.

I halter the black horse and lead him through the corrals to the door of a low-slung barn, which was built by the government after the flood of 1964. Inside the barn is a six-by-twelve-foot tack room that Big John built during my absence in the military. Half a dozen saddles and various horse tack fill the room; thirty-gallon barrels that once held oil for farming tractors sit on wooden pedestals holding the

Joe W. Kipp (Eagle Shoe) in the
middle, sitting with Louis Plenty
Treaty (*left*) and Charley Reevis
(*right*). Courtesy of author.

Isabell Kipp with family friend
Joe Bird Rattler. Cut Bank, Montana, 1958. Courtesy of author.

Hill directly above Kipp home-
stead, the reported site of a reading
by Meriwether Lewis before fighting with the Blackfeet. Courtesy of
author.

Woody Kipp roping calves at
nephew Joe Kipp's ranch on Cut
Bank Creek. Courtesy of author.

(*Left to right*) : Son Daniel, brother
Max, son Munro, and Woody Kipp.
The calf was killed by wild dogs on
the Blackfeet Reservation. Courtesy
of author.

Woody Kipp at the wedding of
a friend. Courtesy of author.

Woody Kipp in Grass Dance outfit,
with face painting of Crazy Dog
Society. Courtesy of author.

saddles. My old saddle is there, given to me by Big John during my sophomore year of high school. It's the kind of saddle that could have been bought for forty dollars in the early years of the century, a saddle that should, given normal circumstances, still be giving good service when the man who bought it is being buried. My saddle has swells that project, that one can get the thighs under; it has a high cantle that puts you down in the saddle, not on top of it, the kind of saddle necessary when big range geldings were the mainstay of horsemen who were working cattle and running horses. It's the kind of saddle my pop rode when he was young, when he rode for the Indian Department herd. There is a notch cut out of one of the skirts in the saddle from when my nephew John Allen and I, as children, made sling shots and cut a piece of the saddle off for the leather slings. We were not lauded for our efforts. Big John's new saddle, by comparison, is sleek and low, a roping saddle without swells, meant for horses that don't buck and for a quick and easy dismount.

The black horse is a full sixteen hands high, weighing in at about eleven hundred pounds. Big John is holding him as I return from the tack room with a snaffle bit, a saddle blanket, and my high-backed saddle. The horse's ears are pointed at me; he snorts and jumps back when I drop the saddle near his head, testing him, seeing how familiar he is with this routine. Big John leads him forward again, toward the saddle sitting on the frozen earth. He snorts at it as if it might bite, an instrument of great suffering.

Big John stands next to the horse's head and holds the lead shank right below the black's jaw. I talk to him and slowly raise the saddle blanket onto his back. He winces a little – the way one might wince with an ice cube on the neck – and then he accepts the blanket. I pick up the saddle, letting it dangle in my hands, and then move it toward his nose. He snorts again, and his front feet brace with his body leaning back, but he doesn't jump. He smells the saddle and accepts that it isn't alive, that it's just leather and wood and rivets and iron rings and the sweat of men and women who have ridden in it. I move to his side with the saddle and push it slowly against his ribs. He flinches. After a few moments of it rubbing against his side, he stands still. I then bring it up, and slowly, carefully, I place the saddle upon his back. Because horses' eyes can see behind them, he can see the stirrup on the off side descending; he again tenses but doesn't jump out from under it. The most ticklish part of the operation begins, getting the cinch tight. Having the barrel enclosed for the first time is a foreign feeling to a horse, the feeling of constriction, of freedom fleeing. Very often a horse that allows a saddle will start bucking at the cinching. With the latigo in the cinch ring, I start pulling the slack out until it touches his side. This must be done slowly, letting the horse adjust to the unaccustomed pressure around his barrel. He flinches, I talk to him, and in a couple of minutes the cinch is snug – not tight, just snug – enough to hold the saddle in place without fear of it turning and draping from his belly if he does move suddenly (a common mistake that traumatizes many good horses). The cinch tightening is where range horses can go ballistic, so I'll pull it tight only just before getting on. I take the lead shank from Big John and buckle the harness around the horse's neck. It's cold, so I hold the iron of the snaffle bit in my hands for half a minute to warm it, so it won't be shockingly cold when it goes into his mouth. I reach up behind his poll and, grabbing the headstall of the bridle, pull the bridle up close to his lips while putting my left thumb in his mouth, pulling down on his lower jaw with my thumb. He opens his mouth, and the bridle is in place, surprising me, as I thought that might be the hardest part of getting him ready. Some horses will stand to be saddled but the bridle is, well, it's a bridle of a whole different color sometimes. When I was sixteen and working for the Consolidated Cattle Company, they had a good palomino horse that had to be tied each morning in order to be bridled. Horses are like people; you run into these little idiosyncrasies and you have to work through them.

The black horse leads easily, though distrustfully, alert, and poised to react. I lead him to the far side of the slab corral and back to where

Big John stands, letting the saddle work into place. Even gentle horses will buck on a cold morning from the cold stiffness of the saddle on their back.

"Well, I guess we're ready," I tell Big John. "Why don't you hold him while I get on, see how he acts."

Big John gets a hold of the bridle reins up close, right under the chin, and when he has a good grip, I step into the stirrup.

I don't get to the off stirrup before the horse's quickness and sheer power – even Big John is no match – has me up over the swells, my face in his mane, and then he throws me in a somersault. I come crashing down to the sub-zero frozen ground on my tailbone, and my spine sizzles. I am really hurt and feel like throwing up. A tailbone smash goes right to the heart, up the spine, into the brain, and you're just plumb hurt.

Standing a few feet away, watching the black buck and admiring the high athletic jumps he's performing, Big John says, "Did you get hurt?"

This is cowboy country. I'm wincing, the pain flares up my backside, and I don't feel like even trying to stand at the moment, but we are conditioned to respond according to who we are or at least who we think we are.

"Nah, I'm okay," I say.

Finally struggling to my feet, I start for the barn, my head swimming from the intense shock of the blow, and I want to sit down. Having bucked to the far side of the corral, the black horse stands there, alert, watching his handiwork hobble away in pain. He's as sleek and lithe as a pinup girl; for me, it takes about a week before I can walk straight again.

I didn't try the black horse again until March. Bill Cadotte, a local cowboy who was helping with the calving, showed me a little trick. Cadotte simply put a catch rope around the black horse's front feet when I went to get on, and he stood still, allowing me into the saddle. Many horses in those days were roped around the front feet and thrown to the ground to be branded. Once a horse becomes aware that by jumping his feet can be taken away and he will end up on the ground, a horse will no longer let his feet leave the ground as long as he feels the rope around his legs. Cowboy physics.

I rode the black horse that spring and learned a lot from him. He helped welcome me back home; it was as close as I would come to a formal ceremony. Riding that black horse, spending time alone out on the prairies as I went about doctoring calves, teaching the horse to rein, roping calves off of him so I could put a pill down their throats to prevent scours, helped me reenter my home in the Blackfeet community. On the back of a spirited black horse, I rode the last leg of my long, meandering trail home from overseas.

After my mom died near the end of that year, Big John and his wife, Bobby, moved into her house in Cut Bank and I stayed on the ranch by myself, working with wild horses, halter-breaking, gentling, saddling, and then mounting. When I had ridden them for a few days in the corral, I would open the main gate and take them to the far part of the connecting corrals, where I would open the adjoining gates and mount at the farthest point from the opened main gate, hoping the horses wouldn't buck me off and bolt through the open front gate.

I was now truly home. The great quietness of the valley on a cold morning with only horses for company was a catharsis from the time I had spent on the streets of Los Angeles and from the things I'd seen in Vietnam. There are some people who have a hard time being alone, but I've never been one of those people – quite the opposite. There is a belief among certain Indian people that if one can't tolerate solitude, there is little chance of becoming a medicine person. Spiritual forces will come to you when you are alone.

I preferred solitude, but like some other Blackfeet men and women, I also liked drinking. By that time, I had become an inveterate drinker and Big John's consumption had also increased. He kept a bottle of vodka in his refrigerator, and after we would finish feeding the cattle, he would tell Bobby to fix us a screwdriver, a mixture of orange juice and vodka. We didn't get drunk, downing only a couple before putting our winter garb back on and going back outdoors. Still, this practice signaled a new openness to drinking in the household, and possibly it reflected an acceptance of me as an adult. Certainly my heavy drinking as a marine leaned right into the screwdrivers.

As I've said, some Blackfeet do like to drink. The bars had opened on our reservation in 1954; the U.S. Congress decided to lift the ban against alcohol on reservations. A big celebration, soon after the ban was lifted, heralded the opening of a couple of bars; I was nine years old and didn't really remember the event. There was an elderly full-blood Blackfeet who had been an accomplished bronc rider but, by the time I was old enough to go into the bars, had been on the streets drinking for many years. A joke told among the Blackfeet cowboys is that this man was cutting hay with a horse-pulled mower out on one of the river bottoms at the time of the opening of the bars. They say – and the story, like many cowboy stories, may be apocryphal – that the old man unhooked his team of horses from the mower, took them to the barn, turned them loose, went into the house for dinner, and then went to town to take part in the opening of the bars. The cowboys say his mower is still sitting right where he unhooked it and he has been on the streets of Browning ever since.

By 1969 drinking had become a way of life for many on the reservation. For those parents in Browning who were drinking, their children had a very limited view of the world. The town was all they knew of the Blackfeet land. I had hunted with my pop all over the reservation as a child, and our great-grandparents had traveled continually during the buffalo days. They knew many things about the region, the northern plains, that has since been lost.

Survival, food and shelter, was not a big concern for the hardcore drinkers in the late-twentieth century; they relied on government surplus foods and the dependability of family. Indians still have a strong sense of the extended family and of kin obligations. Some cousin, uncle, aunt, or good friend will let a drinker in at three in the morning to sleep on the couch or at least on the floor if someone is already on the couch. They'll feed a drinker in the morning and may even loan a couple of bucks to get the drinking day started again. It's nice to walk in the bar and at least have enough money for the first drink.

With drinking comes violence, of course. There were fights in the reservation bars. Lots of fights. Men fighting men. Women fighting women. Women fighting men. People being thrashed by fists and then, after taking a little breather, deciding that an equalizer was in the works and going after the thrasher with a beer bottle, a wine bottle, a whiskey bottle, or maybe a barstool or a pool cue. Years before, glass beer pitchers had been outlawed and replaced by plastic ones, as glass ones made excellent and deadly weapons in a fight. In one instance, the thrashed came back into the bar with a shotgun and put an immediate and violent end to the thrasher.

A buzzer at the front door of a bar permitted the bartender to judiciously decide who could enter and who couldn't. Nearly anyone could get past the buzzer, as long as your name wasn't on a list behind the bar of those who liked to fight and tear the joint up. Consequently, in some bars a husband could get in but the wife couldn't, and at another bar the wife might be permitted to enter but the husband couldn't – husbands and wives drinking in different bars didn't promote marital bliss. A wife managing a peek in a bar and spotting her husband in animated conversation with another woman or, even worse, dancing with someone else would usually result in a rock thrown through the windshield of the family car. As I've said, there are lots of rocks in Blackfeet country. A shattered window of a family sedan is an awfully expensive bit of jealousy come sobriety the next morning.

Some of the places I had been during my Marine Corps days were wild but not wild like the town of Browning, day in and day out. On one memorable drinking day, I was in town in the morning to sign up for unemployment benefits, which I could do upon discharge from the military, and to spend a small unemployment check. I began drinking and continued all day and into the evening, going from the Napi Bar to the Minyard Bar to the Businessmen's Club (a curious name since at that time the only Blackfeet businessmen were the two or three bar owners). I ended up in the Minyard Bar late that night; only a few people remained, most having had a good fill during the day. A couple of older women called to me as I passed by their table and wanted to know who I was. Claiming to have known my biological mother, Lucille, they asked me to sit down and help them finish a pitcher of beer. I was visiting with the women when a young Blackfoot guy stopped at our table and demanded a drink from the pitcher. The women refused, and soon they began arguing. The young man, growing increasingly frustrated, slapped one of the women. Jumping up from the table, I grabbed him and threw him to the floor, going down with him. We wrestled briefly, and since he was quite a bit smaller, I soon had him pinned. He agreed to leave us alone.

It wasn't over. After the women left, I sat at the bar with a guy who introduced himself as John Joseph Yellow Owl, a friend of Big John's who had worked for him as a cowboy. The door opened. Casually glancing in that direction, I saw a very large blond man standing in front of the young guy I had wrestled to the ground. The big blond's name was Dale "Bitsy" Smith. His mother was a half-blood, and his father was a white man – a very large white man – who worked for the county road department driving equipment. I heard my wrestling friend tell Bitsy Smith, "that's him," and a burst of red stars suddenly erupted behind my brain. I found myself on the floor being kicked in the face; I tried getting up but was kicked down again. Having been drinking nearly all day, my chances of getting up from the floor without being further pummeled and kicked were unlikely. I was knocked against the jukebox and took a severe beating as George Jones wailed, "Who's gonna mow your lawn." After a good minute or so of thorough drubbing, they asked if I wanted more. I was smart enough to tell them, no thanks, I've had quite enough for one evening.

I was extremely sore when I woke up at John Joseph Yellow Owl's mother's house the next morning. My lips and face were swollen from kicks and blows, and my ankle was swollen. I just didn't have good sense in those days – when John Joe invited me down for a heal-up-the-hangover drink at the very same bar where I had been knocked silly only twelve hours previously, I accepted. Limping and pained, I retired to the Devil's den once more.

It wasn't the last time. On another occasion, I had drunk all night with a tall cowboy friend of mine, Truman Hall. While waiting for the Napi Bar to reopen at 8:00 a.m. on one spring morning, we went to the Joe Lewis Cafe, run by a full-blood Indian couple, Jim Horn and his wife. His wife wasn't a friendly woman, which didn't do a lot for their business. Still, we weren't looking so much for friendliness as a place to drink till the Napi Bar reopened. Spiking our coffee with whiskey helped, but Jim's wife smelled it and ordered us to leave. After the Napi Bar opened at 8:00 a.m., we ordered a drink. Soon some other Blackfeet came in, some young toughs. A full night of drinking spawns cantankerous attitudes. Before long, one of the young toughs and Truman were battling full tilt. Truman, always ready to fight, was swinging with all his might at the younger, stockier Indian, a half-blood who, unfortunately for Truman, came from a family of Golden Glove champions on the reservation. Truman went down and was kicked. The beating over, he rose and without a word stumbled out the door. The young toughs had another drink and then left. A few minutes later, Truman reappeared at the door, wielding a four-tined pitchfork. He had walked to his sister's house a half mile away and had returned to give some vengeance to his beaters. Luckily they had left, for he wasn't bluffing. I'd seen him fight before and knew his temperament.

A few years later Truman would run into serious trouble in that same bar. Drinking with his brother-in-law, who was also a horseman, they squabbled and fought over something about horses. Earlier, the brother-in-law had had surgery on his intestinal tract and had a tube inserted for medical reasons. After the fight, the brother-in-law had sat in a booth against the wall and apparently passed out with his head on the table. He was dead. The tube had been knocked loose in the fight, and he bled to death sitting there. Truman was charged with manslaughter, but the charge was later dropped.

The reservations are full of these kinds of stories, of Indians surviving but not surviving well because of the disruption of their traditional lifeways. They had become beggars in their own land, where once they were self-sufficient and in control. Indians were already well-versed in the art of horsemanship when white men arrived on the northern plains; we adjusted by becoming a dusky version of the white cowboy, but in so doing, we began terrorizing ourselves as we took on the ways of aggression learned from the white cowboys – the loudmouthed ways, the immorality of booze, the subjugation of our people's ways.

But we can change. That fight with his brother-in-law was Truman's last bout with alcohol. He is a good rancher and a rodeo man, having earlier ridden saddle broncs. After the trauma of the barroom ordeal dissipated, Truman began hosting youth rodeos. The theme behind the youth rodeos was that one doesn't have to be a drinking, fighting, whoring, whiskey-drinking individual to be a cowboy. Truman, like most Blackfeet, is spiritually oriented. His wife attends the Catholic church in Heart Butte, but he saddles a horse and goes to a high hill to pray. The modern Indian – in this case a rancher working stock, running rodeos, pulling horse trailers down the road – still goes back to earlier principles, going alone to meet the Great Mystery.

I farmed and cowboyed for Big John during the summer of 1969. Jean and I stayed in Big John's old house, the one ruined by the flood of 1964 and turned into a combination storage room–bunkhouse. We lived in the big room that had previously been the kitchen and dining room. I hung a large heavy quilt over the door into the other rooms, securing it with small nails.

I remember cutting hay with a swather that summer on Gary Pendergrass's land west of Cut Bank and having a small battery-powered transistor radio that I listened to as I cut the alfalfa. The newscaster said men had landed on the moon.

Late one summer evening, as Jean and I sat talking, a bat that had worked its way around the edge of the hanging quilt started flying around our room. I grabbed a large wooden spoon lying on the old electric stove and chased and killed the bat. A half hour later Big John and a friend of his, the ex–Madison Square Garden bronc rider, Bunny Mutch, pulled into the ranch yard. Bunny Mutch told Jean her father had just called from Valier and that there had been an accident involving her oldest daughter, Desiree. They wanted her to call immediately. We walked to the main house, and when she had been on the phone for a few seconds, I knew something bad had happened. Jean sat down and started crying. Big John took the phone from her. Desi had been riding with some other teenagers around the perimeter of Lake Francis, a manmade lake just on the outskirts of Valier. The driver had slid in the loose gravel of the road, the pickup overturned, and Desi had been killed. The other three teenagers in the back of the truck were injured. We buried Desiree, age sixteen, in the Valier cemetery.

I added to Jean's problems. Drinking heavily one night in Cut Bank, I was heading back to cut hay for Big John when I went to sleep at the wheel of Jean's '59 Chrysler – the Cadillac had died in California – on the Meriwether Road (named for Meriwether Lewis). Missing a culvert by about ten feet, I hit the ditch and totaled Jean's car. Big John gave me a dressing down later – the woman didn't have much money, she had kids to take care of, and here I was, drunk and wrecking her car. My biological mother had not been a responsible person, drinking her life away. Maybe irresponsibility is in the genes.

That fall Jean, who had begun to show her pregnancy, and I moved to the small farm town of Valier, situated about ten miles off of the reservation's southeast corner. Valier is like most little white farm towns, efficient in its own way, exclusive to outsiders. Because many Indians pass through Valier on their way to shop in Great Falls, there was a steady parade of Indians in the Valier bars. Fights between Indians and whites were not uncommon. Because I had grown up around whites in Cut Bank, my attitude toward them was probably somewhat different than many of the Indians who passed through and stopped to drink. Many Indians have never socialized with white people outside of the barroom setting, and that setting itself is not always so jovial.

By October we were pretty broke, except for the welfare money Jean received for her daughters. Odd jobs helped us survive. I had heard of a man, Rib Gustafson, a veterinarian in the town of Conrad, which was twenty miles from Valier, who needed straw bales picked from the field and hauled and stacked. Gustafson didn't have a vehicle with which to pull a trailer, so we used Jean's next car, a '59 Chevy sedan purchased from Truman Hall. She drove, I loaded and stacked the bales, and then we hauled them to the straw stack. In early December I went to work for Louie DeBoo, taking care of his cows east of Heart Butte on Blacktail Creek. The next spring in 1970 I went to work for Norwegian farmers, Ronald and Lawrence Nelson, who treated me well.

While working for the Nelson brothers in Valier, my friends and I had run some hippies out of town for wearing strange clothes and having long hair and because we couldn't beat them at pool. Soon those clothes, that hair, and the hippie culture would become commonplace for me.

Understanding

9

With jobs sporadic and money scarce, it was time for us to explore other options. In 1970, Jean (now my wife and the mother of our baby girl) and I applied and were accepted to the University of Montana. At twenty-six, I had been accepted under the provisions of the GI Bill as a result of my Vietnam service. In late August, while I was still farming for the Nelson brothers, Jean and the girls went to Missoula and rented a small house. The next week we loaded a U-Haul, she and the girls went to Missoula to get settled in, and I continued to farm until mid-September. I didn't know the first thing about going to college. Reaching Missoula, I bought what I thought were college clothes – slacks and sports shirts – and my cowboy clothes went into storage. Not long after we started school, the owner of the house we were renting sold the place, and we rented a large, very nice house just two blocks from campus. We recouped the more expensive rent by sub-letting four basement rooms.

It was with some trepidation that I attended my first classes. The Native Studies Department at the University of Montana was young, having begun a couple of years earlier, and was operated out of a row of houses adjacent to campus that had been private residences until the university had purchased them. For most of the Indian students, college was their first day-to-day social contact with white people; for me, it was my first time around a gaggle of Natives in an educational setting.

I decided I would try my hand at writing. Nobody in my family had ever written; none had ever been inveterate readers except me. My family was of the plains and mountains, reading the land directly, reading tracks, wind, and the ears of horses. The only reading or writing they did on a continuing basis was horse and cattle brands and the signing of an occasional check. I knew how to write a complete sentence, even if I didn't always understand the mechanics of grammar.

Native students often encounter difficulty in freshman English classes at mainstream universities. The University of Montana, recognizing this problem, organized a special English class just for Native students. Dr. Brown, the professor of that class, called me aside one day after we had written an exposition of Camus' *The Wind at Jemilla*. He said he really liked the writing I had done and asked if I had ever considered going to law school. I hadn't.

Dr. Brown sparked an acrimonious debate in class by bringing up a story about the morality of hunting. He most likely had eaten out of grocery stores for quite some time; his hands hadn't touched the warm blood of the kill for a while. The story brought a loud and argumentative response from the Native students. For the most part, they didn't respond well to the usual class materials, but the hunting issue was close to home, close to their deep cultural ties, close to the blood and hide that had been their survival for millennia. They defended hunting, as did I.

I also became more aware of the pervasive inequalities in American society and how the challenges confronting Indians were bound up with those of other races and cultures. One literature class, taught by a middle-aged white woman, examined the novels of black novelist and Pulitzer Prize winner Toni Morrison. I challenged the professor's assertion that Black literature was distinctive from other forms of American literature because of slavery; in my view, Blacks and Indians spoke to similar themes in their stories and narratives, owing to the shared condition of white supremacy.

Many of the students – mainly young, liberal white women – agreed with the distinctions between Native and Black literatures sketched out by the professor. One young, pudgy Jewish woman, attempting to identify with atrocities committed against people of color, pointed to the discrimination against those who are overweight. While agreeing with the possibility of prejudice, I argued that the consequences were not the same in such a case: one would not be murdered or lynched for being overweight.

I enjoyed the campus consciousness and started to understand being Indian from an academic angle. I began to see that much had been written about me and my people, and a lot was utter bullshit, written by white males who never found or knew themselves spiritually, so the writing they did about others, about Indians, was flawed from the outset.

While becoming wiser in some ways, I still had much to learn in others. I was not a good husband, and I didn't know much about being a father. The Blackfeet were efficient as hunters, horsemen, and fighters, but the gentle side of tribal life had been stolen away by John Wayne's predecessors. My adopted father, Eagle Shoe, as I have said, was unsympathetic; I don't remember any of the men in my family ever saying I love you to their wives, to their children, or to anyone. It just wasn't done. My own daughter was an infant, and I was spending a great deal of time away from her, Jean, and the other girls, doping, drinking, and sometimes whoring.

The University of Montana campus in the fall of 1971 was full of young people with raggedy clothes and long, unkempt hair. I was soon caught up in their fast lifestyle, often staying out partying with friends till the wee hours, and sometimes I didn't go home all weekend. I had tried smoking dope in Vietnam once, but it didn't seem to do anything for me. One night some young white people invited me to a house party. Upon my suggestion one of them, a man with a massive black beard, drove my car, since he knew the location of the party. At the party somebody pulled out a bong, the first I'd ever seen, and began giving people nose hits. They gave me a hit, and in a few minutes I was flying. The high was at first exhilarating, but soon paranoia settled in. I began to feel that I should get away from these people, that danger lurked in the old apartment building in which we sat. The heavily bearded driver, however, had put my car keys in his pocket, and I was afraid to ask for them. Sitting across the room from me, he seemed to take on the aura of the now infamous Charles Manson. At my request someone finally asked the bearded driver for my keys. He flashed a friendly smile to me from across the room and handed the keys over.

Despite this harrowing mental experience, I soon became a regular dope smoker, hanging out with the hippies and learning their lingo. Conservatism born of cowboy life, Catholicism, the Marine Corps, and a small-town boyhood began dropping away like old snakeskin. Not long before, I had run hippies out of Valier; now I was in the middle of them, holding court.

By 1971 I had also become fast friends and drinking buddies with Jean's ex-brother-in-law, King Kuka, an art student at the university. We would retire to a trailer house owned by a Blackfoot woman on the west side of Missoula, far from the campus, where we would party with booze, dope, and whomever we had been able to lure out of the local bars. The drunken revelry eventually culminated in a bizarre, but I guess successful, moose-hunting expedition to the Bitterroot Mountains. We drank, killed a moose, got lost, got stuck, misplaced our food and booze, partook of illicit romance, and I fell into an icy cold mountain creek.

It seemed liked hellacious fun at the time, but I would live that part of my life differently if I could do it again.

I continued to grow in understanding. Drinking, doping, and whoring did not prevent me from absorbing concepts and new kinds of information that I had never heard discussed before. Abstractions mouthed in grade school and high school – liberty, justice, equality – were scrutinized and discussed at length by the hippie acquaintances. My Vietnam experience threw some of these concepts into sharp relief. I was coming into a different sense of who I was as a minority member in America, something I had always known but had never understood in depth. It was always there, and I lived with it, knowing that the white people had a less-than-wholesome opinion of my race.

This incipient learned wisdom rose to the surface and took firm hold in the summer of 1972. The U.S. government had paid the Blackfeet for a large parcel of land that we were forced to surrender last century. Everybody received a couple of thousand dollars; Jean and I used our money to buy a fairly nice car, a 1967 Pontiac. Jean and I also took our girls to the Arlee powwow on the Flathead reservation. That powwow heralded the end of one way of thinking about the world and the beginning of a new trail.

Joining
10

After setting up our camp at the Arlee powwow, Jean and I participated in the festivities. She went off to play the ancient Indian gambling game, which in my part of the country is called either hand game or stick game. Players sit in two lines facing one another, singing Native songs, and trying to guess who has the marked bone. Sometimes big stakes can be won. I went to the beer garden, which was set up about a hundred yards away from the arbor, where the traditional Native dancers were to perform. The fact that a beer garden had been set up within the powwow grounds at Arlee speaks to the misguided and wrongheaded thinking Indian people had been led into, being convinced that drinking like a white man constituted some kind of cultural advance.[1] In a couple of years the powwow beer garden would vanish as a revitalized cultural consciousness raced through Indian country, upsetting much of what had been taken for granted in the previous century. Today, I would throw anybody drinking off powwow grounds.

I ran into Curly Bear Wagner and Ray Spang at the Arlee powwow. They too were drinking and began talking about an organization they had joined called the American Indian Movement, which had been founded in 1968 in Minneapolis. Curly Bear is Blackfoot; Ray is a Northern Cheyenne, whose hair, even when braided, reached well past his waist. Curly Bear was just starting to grow his hair out and wore short braids wrapped with red cloth, a contemporary symbol of the AIM warriors. Curly Bear had been quite a good athlete on the Blackfeet reservation, in football a running back and in track a sprinter who went to the state meet. We graduated from high school at about the same time, and he married a white woman from Browning (by 1972 the marriage had ended). We are blood related through the genealogy of Hugh Munro and his familial connections to the Blood chief Red Crow.

Curly Bear and Ray began telling me about treaty rights, civil rights, Native religion, and the Alcatraz protests. The radicalism among Natives had started a decade earlier, with the appearance on the national Indian scene of people such as Clyde Warrior, but I had never heard Indians discuss such issues in detail. Ray Spang and Curly Bear Wagner and a couple of other Indian activists had formed an AIM chapter in Billings. I came to know the original AIM members: Frank Lamere, a Winnebago from Nebraska; Dennis Decoteau, a Sisseton Dakota; and T.R. Yellowtail, a Crow whose grandfather had been influential in Montana politics. They invited me to attend an AIM meeting in Fort Robinson, Nebraska, in mid-September of that year. During the four days of the Arlee powwow, I became convinced they were more than just bullshitting; they had cards with the name American Indian Movement printed on them and a place for a member to sign. I took a card and signed, not at all sure of the implications of doing so, but I would soon learn.

Shortly after meeting Curly Bear and Ray Spang at the Arlee pow-wow, I had my hair cut for the last time at a little barbershop across the street from the University of Montana campus. I've never had my hair cut since, except for an involuntary trim when one of my braids got caught in a rock-drilling machine, which happened while I was working for the Forest Service after returning to the university in 1987.

A couple of weeks after I joined AIM, two VISTA (Volunteers in Service to America) women came to work in the Community Action Program (CAP) in Missoula. One was a tall blonde from Soddy Daisy,

Tennessee, and the other was an Indian woman from Tama, Iowa. The CAPs were federal anti-poverty programs designed to help the poor pull themselves up by their bootstraps. Jim Parker, a good man who ran the program in Missoula, asked if I would help welcome the new VISTA workers at a picnic. Within a couple of weeks I was in bed with the blonde; soon Curly Bear was seeing the Indian woman from Iowa, who later would become pregnant and miscarry. The VISTA women had no qualms about helping organize an AIM meeting. None of the local AIM men were married, and I acted like I wasn't either. From the start, the movement fostered a kind of cavalier attitude toward everyday life, as if we were traveling at a place above or outside of those conventions. None of us had any money; none had nine-to-five jobs; my family's only support was the school payments from my GI Bill.

I did a lot of coyote kind of ducking and diving in those days, being married and all. My wife, Jean, knew I was going to the forthcoming AIM meeting at Fort Robinson and assumed my car, an old Mercury Comet recently purchased from a white farmer, would be stored at the bus depot. Wanting to spend a night with the VISTA woman before leaving, however, I left my car in her garage. The blonde drove me to the bus depot early the next morning and dropped me off to wait for the bus. Arriving in Billings, I was picked up by Curly Bear and Frank Lamere, and we spent the night at Frank Lamere's place. The next day, we left Billings for Fort Robinson in a big station wagon owned by T.R. Yellowtail's girlfriend, Jeri.

Practicing that do-as-we-say-not-as-we-do AIM ideology, we drank lime vodka when we left Billings. T.R. was driving, and was driving fast – about ninety. It was a big car with a powerful engine; our high on lime vodka didn't diminish our deadly sense of speed, too much speed. Dennis Decoteau moved into the far back part of the station wagon and put the sleeping bags in front of him in an attempt to create a cushion in case T.R. lost control on a curve.

We arrived.

The day after we made it to Fort Robinson, some of the AIM leaders and elders, including spiritual leader Leonard Crow Dog, who would gain international fame during the Wounded Knee siege the following year, met to discuss the death of Richard Oakes, a Native activist who only a couple of weeks earlier had been murdered by a white man in California. A cross-country trip to Washington DC had been hinted at previously, and the death of Oakes, well respected among the movers and shakers in Native circles, cemented the idea. At a large gathering, we listened to speeches about various aspects of the movement and what should be done; we heard elders talk of a history of unaddressed injustices. The speakers berated the elected tribal councils as lackeys of the government.

When the meeting ended in the late afternoon, our alcoholism demanded attention, and we went to a small farm-and-ranch town a few miles from Fort Robinson. Four of us entered a bar in the cow town, one sporting extremely long hair, two with moderately long hair past their shoulders, and me – I was just starting to grow my hair out. It was a typical western saloon, a long forty-foot bar on one side and tables against the wall on the other side. Four cowboys sat at one of the tables. This time I was a longhair invading the space of cowboys. We were no more than seated at the bar when one of the cowboys spoke up.

"Wanna borrow a comb?" He was used to the old style of Indian, those they had been dealing with since the reservations had been created.

Spinning around on his barstool, Dennis Decoteau looked the cowboy in the eyes and told him, "No, thanks, I've got my own comb." We could see them in the mirror behind the bar.

The cowboys went back to talking among themselves after Dennis fired back at them. We drank one beer and ordered another. It had been a long day away from the booze. A Chihuahua lapdog, belonging to T.R.'s girlfriend, sat outside the door of the bar, waiting.

One of the cowboys walked outside. We could hear him cuss the dog, and then the Chihuahua yelped, as if kicked. In a flash T.R. was off his stool and out the door; we climbed off our stools and followed, the other cowboys rising from their table and also heading for the door. When we reached the sidewalk, the cowboy who had kicked T.R.'s dog was lying in the gutter, knocked completely out. One of the cowboys ran over and kneeled by him as the man started to come to. The kneeling cowboy screamed at the top of his voice, "You fuckin' cheapskate Indians!" (I'm not sure why he was using that particular terminology, as there hadn't been anything economic about our transaction.) The other cowboys yelled into the bar for the bartender to call the cops.

That call escalated into trouble we weren't ready to face. We knew what dealing with small-town white cops meant, so somebody grabbed T.R.'s dog, and we quickly got into our car. The big station wagon had power steering, and in our haste to get the hell out of there before the cops showed up, T.R. cut the steering a bit too sharply backing out. We hooked onto the bumper of the car next to us and started pulling it into the street. Quickly disengaging the cars, we fled, our beers untouched.

In that encounter at the cow town bar, Cowboys and Indians fought, but with a twist – the Indians had once been cowboys and were now going back to being Indians, but the cowboys had never been Indians and never would be.[2]

That night at the AIM meeting at Fort Robinson, I first glimpsed internal dissension between spiritual leaders of different tribes. T.R. Yellowtail verbally attacked and challenged Leonard Crow Dog, telling him that he wasn't afraid of his Yuwipi medicine, that he had his own Coyote medicine.

I understood the concept of Indian medicine, of spiritual power, but it was a historical understanding. As a young boy, when I rode horseback with my pop, he'd tell me stories from the past, like this one: A band of Blackfeet horse raiders were being pursued by the enemy they had stolen horses from the night before. In a grove of trees in a gully, they made a stand and killed several of the enemy before the enemy gave up the fight and retired. One of the enemy had a good repeating rifle lying near him, and when one of the Blackfeet raiders approached him, the body moved. Assuming the man was wounded but still alive, he fired another bullet into the body. After he fired, the body kept moving, and he fired again. The body twisted as it moved, and when the chest of the man was visible, he could see that the man wore a bandolier made from the skin of a rattlesnake. By this time some other Blackfeet men had drawn near and were watching the twisting man. Again the raider fired, to no avail; the body kept moving. The Blackfeet gathered their spoils and quickly left. Nobody was willing to go near the man's rattlesnake medicine body. They left the rifle.

Although I had heard these stories as a child, they were historically situated; in my mind they were tales of the past. So when T.R. Yellowtail challenged Leonard Crow Dog, it was new to me – potent Indian medicine in the present. I was reminded of T.R.'s challenge to Crow Dog when I learned that T.R.'s brother had been trying to start a car by priming it with gasoline – the engine backfired, burning his face.

I was broke except for a few dollars when we returned to Billings in the late evening. My AIM brothers promised me money the following day, but I didn't feel like waiting another day in Billings. I decided to hitchhike to Missoula. Accompanied by a pint of whiskey, at 10:00 p.m. I began walking in the chilly, but not cold, night. At about two or three in the morning, a Volkswagen Beetle stopped and a guy from Bozeman gave me a ride all the way to that town. My meager funds bought me only a short breakfast, so I was soon back on the freeway, hitchhiking. A teenager gave me a ride to the Three Forks area, followed by a young white hippie couple with New Jersey plates who gave me a ride as far as Butte. I got off downtown, and after a day's walk of nearly twenty miles with a hangover, called Jean in Missoula to come pick me up. She appeared in a couple of hours; during the ride back to Missoula, she asked about the meeting in Fort Robinson but didn't say much else.

My affair had been discovered. Unbeknownst to me, while I was gone, a young people's party was held at the home where my VISTA woman was staying. Murna Boyd, a very vocal Indian woman activist from Fort Peck, had asked Jean to help chaperone. During the course of the party, some of the chaperones, noticing the wobbly gaits of the partygoers, suspected drinking. When a teenager fell down in the attached garage, too drunk to walk, the chaperones – including Jean – went into the garage to see what was happening. There, a very familiar old Mercury Comet sat.[3]

Jean got her revenge. After returning to Missoula, the local AIM members held a meeting at the house of the VISTA women. Afterward, the blonde wanted to go to a bar downtown called Jekyll and Hydes to listen to a band. As soon as we pulled away from her house, a parked car behind us turned on its lights. I immediately recognized the configuration of the headlights as belonging to the Pontiac Jean and I had bought. When I told the VISTA woman I was sure Jean was following, she moved over to the far passenger side. Once off the residential street and onto a main street, the Pontiac came up directly behind us – there was no doubt that my wife had us dead to rights.

I pulled into the parking lot of a small convenience store, telling the blonde to inform my wife if confronted that we were simply buying cigarettes for the guys at the AIM meeting. The deception didn't have a chance. As the blonde walked toward the store, Jean pulled up and met her at the door, cussing her out and taking a swing at her. The blonde ran back toward me, but Jean caught her just as she was in front of the car, grabbing her hair and trying to hit her. They fell toward the rear of the car, the blonde striking her forehead on the rearview mirror, breaking it off. She then ran into the darkness of a vacant lot next to the convenience store.[3] Jean and I argued, and she stormed off, threatening to come back with my .308 hunting rifle.

Back at the VISTA house, I discovered the door locked; Curly Bear cautiously moved the curtain aside to see who had knocked. He let me in and asked what had happened, saying the blonde had come in crying, with a knot on her forehead the size and color of a plum. I told him what had happened and that my wife had threatened to return with a rifle. The AIM members reacted by continuing to drink beer and smoke weed while playing cards at the kitchen table. A fairly large window faced the street, so every time a car was heard, they'd duck just in case a bullet came through the window. We were too stoned to realize that a low shot could just as easily go through the side of the house.

Jean called the VISTA office the following day and told the VISTA supervisor of the infidelity, threatening to shoot the woman if she wasn't out of town immediately. That ended the affair.[4]

Occupying

//

In the fall of 1972, eight national Indian organizations, including AIM, met and decided to form a caravan, dubbed the Trail of Broken Treaties, which would cross the country from California to Washington DC in order to protest treaty rights violations and other issues. The leaders behind the movement felt that arriving in the nation's capital right before the November presidential elections would be sure to attract media attention, raise visibility for Indian issues, and perhaps win some concessions. Leaders of AIM visited reservations, campuses, and other Indian gathering places across the country to drum up support for the caravan.

In early September 1972 a sign at the Native Studies building at the University of Montana announced a forthcoming presentation by an Indian man named Russell Means. I had never heard of Russell Means but the meeting looked interesting, so a couple of friends and I attended. Means wore his hair in braids, in the manner of the old-timers. His appearance was striking, as was the fervor and intensity of his message. Means talked about the rights of Indian people, speaking of the political, legal, social, and cultural rights of Native peoples as being something that we, as university students, should be aware of and doing something about. He then mentioned a caravan, the Trail of Broken Treaties, that would be coming through Missoula in about a month's time. Means convinced the Native Studies Director, Henrietta Whiteman, that students should be allowed to travel with the caravan as an educational experience.

Whiteman, having come from that hot corner of the world that was the Berkeley campus of the 1960s, was receptive to the proposal. A few days after Means's departure, Henrietta Whiteman made arrangements for the seventeen students who had signed up for the trip to get university credit; the students would keep daily journals and give presentations to various classes upon their return. The credits were given through the departments of Native Studies, Sociology, and Political Science. We approached Indian organizations in Missoula and the surrounding areas and came up with twenty-eight hundred dollars, enough to buy a few used cars for the trip. A package deal from a used car dealer in Missoula resulted in three used automobiles. In 1972 you could buy a fairly good used car for about a thousand dollars.

We consequently were able and willing to join the Trail of Broken Treaties caravan when it traveled through Missoula in early October. As it had been doing all along, the caravan visited reservations, stopping at Crow and Northern Cheyenne after we joined. At each stop, informational meetings took place. Like me, nearly all Indians at that time were quite ignorant of the implications of treaty rights and the obligations that were taken on by the federal government when the treaties were signed. The public school system, the churches, and the media had worked their dark magic upon us.

After passing through small South Dakota towns like Winner, Wagner, and Yankton, a group of us went to the Sisseton reservation in northeast South Dakota, the birthplace of my friend, Dennis Decoteau. We met with the tribal chairman, Moses Gill, who supported the caravan, offering a school bus to haul some young people.[1]

That evening, we retired to a watering hole in Sisseton where several of the locals were gathered, listening to Dennis Decoteau describe the purpose of the Trail of Broken Treaties. After a few drinks and the powerful words being spoken by my friend, a half dozen listeners showed definite interest in going, including a man and his sister. The sister, sitting across the table from me and very attractive, had shoulder-length black hair and was dressed cowgirl style; when she rose to use the ladies room, I noticed she really filled her pair of Wranglers. Suddenly finding my voice, I began building the Indian cowgirl a few sandcastles despite my limited knowledge of the ideology of the movement. We soon began a riotous, eventually bittersweet, affair.

Upon reaching Minneapolis–St. Paul, we found that the caravan had grown considerably. The organizers had decided to stay in the Twin Cities for a few days in order to draft a twenty-point proposal for federal Indian policy reform to present to officials in Washington DC and to hold educational workshops for participants in the caravan. Over the next few days, I learned about the Little Red School House, operated by AIM in St. Paul. Its students were politicized at an early age – children in the first grade knew more about treaty rights than many of the adults traveling with the caravan. They were being taught to sing on a drum and understand the meaning behind the drum. They were cracking the facade of false white male history concerning this country and how it had been formed.

And we also were taught. For days we participated in workshops on the upcoming meetings with federal officials. Those of us who had been politically uninformed began to become conversant in what a treaty *really* was. Like many others at that time, I understood treaties in the frontier context of John Wayne movies, in which a treaty stood as an obstacle to rightful action by the white hero. The western movies taught us that nothing could or should be resolved, except for which white woman would sigh and ride off into the sunset with John Wayne. Our attitude became, Fuck John Wayne and all that he stands for.

Being around AIM leaders like Russell Means, Dennis Banks, and the Belcourt brothers, Vernon and Clyde, was very instructive for me. They carried themselves with a certain confidence, a pronounced arrogance that one recognized as having come from pushing themselves forward into the world as Native men battling for something that was theirs. That confidence galvanized and lent strength to protests, including one that occurred while we were in the Twin Cities. When a report came in that Indian students were being discriminated against in the St. Paul public school system, a contingent of AIM people approached the school in question with the intent of talking to the administration. One of the main mottos of AIM was that its people were bound by the bond of the drum. That belief was put into practice. We entered the school building behind the large AIM drum, the singers singing at full tilt.

The mandate of sobriety for members of the movement proved hard to handle. The Sisseton cowgirl and I frequently left the caravan to visit her relatives in the Twin Cities, where we would drink, smoke dope, and lapse into our everyday selves. (She was a spitfire when she'd had a few drinks, and within a couple of weeks we were already having lovers' spats.) A devil-may-care mood infected the caravan, a cavalier attitude that came from knowing we were on the verge of something – we weren't quite sure just what. Something our parents hadn't done; something that hadn't been done in quite a while. The history that had been hidden was seeping out.

Soon we were all called together to talk about the drinking done by the Montana contingent and some of the AIM leaders. Carter Camp delivered a longwinded lecture about sobriety that was met with downcast stares by the Montana group; we knew we were guilty. Fractures within AIM – the threat of increasing separation by state or by tribe – had already started taking place and would worsen as tribal and individual egos continued to inflate.

By the time the caravan left for Washington DC, those who had sat through sessions dealing with legal affairs had become aware that there was a part of the U.S. Constitution that mentioned treaties and that, in the legal construct of America as a land of laws and not men, we had legal standing. The Twenty Point Proposal was drafted, a proposal that we hoped would embarrass and get the attention of the Nixon administration on the eve of the November elections.

As we made our way from the Twin Cities to the nation's capital, I was twenty-seven years old; most of the Indian students from the University of Montana were younger. The bulk of the caravan members were also young, but there were some elders and quite a few middle-aged people who accompanied us to Washington DC. I was having a good time and had taken on the euphoric air of a revolutionary – near-tantric sex, good smoke, an occasional sneaked beer, and a purpose in life. Our car, filled with my fellow revolutionaries, was running well. I was learning a new way of being an American, a new way of being Indian.

The cars comprising the caravan represented Indian economic life – some were okay, but the others were in really rough condition with cracked windshields, no mufflers, bald tires, or doors held closed with rope. The better cars in the caravan included our three used cars bought in Missoula. At least a couple of the old reservation cars gave out as they strained to keep their passengers at freeway speed; we abandoned them, and the riders loaded into other cars.

Approaching Washington DC, some five hundred strong, we were met on the city's outskirts by state troopers and highway patrol, who had been apprised of our approach. At about 4:00 a.m., motorcycle cops and squad cars led us to the White House, our announced first stop. The whole caravan debarked there along with the big AIM drum. Outside the fence surrounding the White House we sang the national anthem of AIM. We had wanted to let Nixon know we were in town, but sadly he was up north at Camp David, so he didn't hear our early morning serenade to the American Dream.

Piling back into our cars, we went to the place where we would stay while meeting with federal officials about our treaty rights. Located in an impoverished part of the city, the building was an old, disemboweled, empty church. It had no amenities, not even running water. Somebody claimed to have seen rats in the building when we arrived, an announcement that sent a shock wave through the crowd. Many felt that we might be subject to a rat attack while sleeping, a fear amplified by a *Washington Post* front-page story that day of a child bitten by a rat in the city.[2]

After milling around in the abandoned church, we held a meeting. Someone suggested that we go to the BIA headquarters and tell the people who ran our lives that we needed help in finding a suitable place to stay while we met with federal officials. Back into our cars we went, wending our way through the city streets to the BIA building. Arriving at about the beginning of the workday, we parked as many cars as would fit into the parking lot of the BIA building and spilled over the rest into the surrounding streets. I was feeling a little hung over as we entered the domain of the high and mighty people who ran the country – the previous night we had pulled on a quart of something – vodka, I think.

Indians soon filled a large auditorium in the BIA building. Because the caravan media people had alerted the Washington press, news teams soon began streaming into the building. Native peoples from all parts of the country began shooting questions at Harrison Loesch and John Crow, highly placed officials in the Department of the Interior, who were bathed in the bright lights of the media teams. Questions about timber, water, land, mineral rights, civil rights, criminal cases – all manner of concerns about the lives of Indians – flew at the bureaucrats, who fended off inquiries by expressing uncertainty about specific cases, which, they promised, would be investigated.

Right.

I remember Harrison Loesch, bald, sweating profusely while being hammered by an old lady from Oklahoma about massive corruption in her homeland. Although he listened, from where I sat it was apparent he wished to be elsewhere – in his plush office up the street at Interior – instead of standing in front of bright lights answering to hostile Indians. We had nothing to lose in the political milieu of Washington DC and possibly had much to gain if we could get answers, get light shined into dark and nefarious reservation corners, which had not been lit in a long time.

The BIA building was massive, a small city. At noon we ate in the basement cafeteria and then continued to grill the bureaucrats. By midafternoon our hangovers were pretty thirsty. My cousin, one of the students from the University of Montana, knew an Indian woman who was a law student at a college in DC. He called her and asked for the use of her apartment; she willingly opened up the apartment and told us to help ourselves to food, showers, whatever. A carload of us then left the droning meeting in the BIA building and went to freshen up, bringing along a case of beer to help the process. We spent about an hour or more at the woman's apartment, showering, toking up, and drinking some cold beer.

At five o'clock that afternoon, while we were away from the building, the bureaucrats, in the time-honored manner of their kind, announced it was time to go home; they would return at nine the next morning and the questioning could resume then. The leadership of our caravan apprised the bureaucrats that there were about a thousand Indians in the building who needed adequate housing while the meetings continued. Apparently rejecting the request, the bureaucrats, amidst heated debate, ordered the security forces of the building to start escorting Indians outside. The Indians resisted, saying they would camp right there in the auditorium. When the security guards attempted to physically oust some Indians, violence erupted and the bureaucrats, security forces, and attendant BIA personnel were rapidly thrown out of the building by Indians.

We returned a few minutes after this forced exodus occurred, ignorant to what had taken place but also aware of a large contingent of city police officers arriving. Someone shouted at us from a window on the first floor, which is recessed into the ground. It was Browneyes, a big, tall Lakota guy, yelling at us to try and get into the building.

The cops were standing in formation, numbering around fifty. A racial tinge to their makeup was immediately apparent – all were black except the officer in charge. I walked over to the white commander and asked why all the police here were black. He was polite enough, explaining that the inner city of DC was about 90 percent black. I accepted his answer and returned to where Browneyes was looking out the window. He moved some furniture that had been shoved in front for blockage, and we squeezed our way in.

Once in, there wasn't much for me to do but roam the building and find the Sisseton cowgirl. She and I roamed the upper reaches of the BIA headquarters, looking for a nest. We deposited our scant belongings behind the big mahogany desk of some high-flying BIA official, in effect taking up residence there. The carpet was nice and thick. I noticed that there were a number of elderly in the building, as well as women, children, and even some babies, since the mothers hadn't known an occupation was going to take place.

Rumors flew that the cops were preparing to assault the building. Not in the inner circle of leadership, I hung out with the warriors. A quick assessment of the resources at hand yielded makeshift weapons from such places as a maintenance shop in the basement. We took big hardwood table legs and fitted them into a large vise mounted on a bench. Once in the vise, twenty-penny nails were driven through the large end of the table legs, making quite formidable clubs. At least a few of the AIM warriors carried more conventional weapons.

We assumed that gas would be shot into the building, so women of the caravan tore up pieces of t-shirts, or whatever else could soak up water, and placed buckets of water at each recessed ground window, where a half dozen warriors waited with their ungainly clubs. If gassed, we had been instructed to dip a piece of cloth in the bucket of water and hold it to our noses while using the other hand to swing the club.

No attack came.

I learned that the commissioner of Indian Affairs, Louis Bruce, had chosen to stay in the building with us instead of fleeing with the other bureaucrats. We really enjoyed hearing that bit of news. In a telephone statement to the press, Bruce explained that he stayed because we were the people he was hired to represent. Bravo, Louis. He would later be fired for this stance, but we'll remember his heroic act. Although he would soon leave the building on the orders of his superiors, Bruce bolstered the morale of the caravan members considerably by standing with us in the early hours of the occupation.

When we originally sealed the building, the main entryway, a big set of glass doors, was barricaded with all manner of heavy things – desks, tall filing cabinets, display cases. After the first night, those objects were removed and we went out into the front part of the building freely; there was always, however, a gaggle of warriors stationed near the doors, ready to secure them if the need arose. At the top of each flight of stairs waited a large pile of Selectric typewriters, each about forty pounds, to be dropped as bombs on anyone storming the stairwells. We also lifted by rope a couple of sets of tipi poles to the roof. The tipis were originally intended to be set up on the lawn of the BIA building for symbolic display while we met with officials. They now became weapons, positioned directly over the entrance where the poles could be speared down upon the Philistines. Indian kind of thinking, brutal and effective.

In subsequent days the occupation proved similar to my Vietnam experience – long stretches of boredom punctuated by periods of frantic activity as deadlines for evacuation neared and evaporated. At one point, a rumor of an imminent helicopter assault on the roof took hold. We waited there, determined to fight if it did come. Rumors of another attack swept the caravan members about five days after the takeover. By that point, the strain of the ordeal and enforced sobriety had tautened tolerance to bowstring levels. We moved cans of gasoline (siphoned from caravan cars) to the upper floors of the building and sent word to the enemy's leaders that an assault would precipitate the torching of the building. Most of the people of the caravan weren't allowed anywhere on the upper floors at that time. It was tense.

Crowded and living on top of one another, sometimes we were our own worst enemies. At one point, someone found a coffeemaker on one of the upper floors, so I went to get some coffee. Carrying two Styrofoam cups full of very hot coffee, I backed slowly out of the room into the stairwell; the door closed before I realized that the light bulb had burned out. Hot coffee in both hands, I carefully felt my way down the pitch-black stairs. Alas, a young couple was embracing on the second set of stairs, apparently so engaged they hadn't noticed the door opening above them. I tripped over them, spilling coffee on their heads. Their sudden screams nearly scared me to death, and we all fell down the stairs. It was horrific.

And while we waited to fight, Sacred Pipe ceremonies were held daily by the more knowledgeable members of the caravan, notably Leonard Crow Dog, who by that time had assumed the role of the spiritual leader of AIM. As a former marine, I considered myself a warrior and didn't readily make a connection between warfare and spirit. I carried a big oak table leg with a dangerous nail sticking out its end. I was warfare. Those who prayed, who held traditional Indian ceremonies, impressed me, but I hadn't been raised around the Sacred Pipe; I had eaten the flesh and had drunk the blood of the Holy Christ through the ceremonies of the Catholic Church. Something deep within me, though, did recognize the importance of the people who were praying with the Sacred Pipe, but that recognition wouldn't surface and take form until several months later on the Pine Ridge Reservation, just before taking part in another occupation.

During the occupation political people, such as Stokely Carmichael, the black militant, came and offered their support. Various civil rights groups from the DC area brought us food and other supplies. A group of Indians from North Carolina also appeared a couple of days into the occupation. They didn't mingle much with us; we were mostly from the American West. Many of us, not familiar with eastern seaboard history, thought the North Carolina visitors were black people. Someone explained the long history of intermarriage between blacks and Indians in that part of the country.

After a week the occupation of the BIA headquarters was declared over on November 8. The White House had agreed to pay for us to return home and not to prosecute the occupiers of the BIA building.

More important, they had agreed to establish an interagency task force that would meet with different Indian organizations and address our grievances and ideas. We left the BIA building and went to the YMCA. I learned later that certain caravan members took with them boxes of BIA files containing what some called incriminating evidence. They spirited the records out at night, under cover of darkness, loading them into the trunks of cars parked in the BIA parking lot.

We left the city in a triumphant mood and headed back to the Twin Cities, where we were to rejoin the other caravan members for a victory celebration. With the occupation behind us, and enjoying a sense of victory over bungling bureaucrats, we immediately regressed and started drinking. Although a large contingent of the caravan was traveling together on the return trip, my friends deliberately chose not to travel with the large caravan. Buzzed on the way, as someone had scored marijuana before leaving Washington DC, we drank, smoked, and recounted our bizarre introduction to the world of treaty politics. Somebody missed a freeway exit during the night, and we ended up the next morning in Ohio. We did eventually reach the Twin Cities.

A large party ensued at a Minneapolis bar, the victory mood embellished by a sense of rebellion against white authority. Because we wouldn't leave the bar at closing time, a large force of cops appeared and forced us to return to our rooms at the Holiday Inn in Minneapolis. The victory party continued there, and we woke the following morning hung over but with new political insight.

The Sisseton cowgirl did not accompany me back to Montana. We had had a spat during the occupation, and by this time she was running with Russell Means. I had some deep feelings for her that took a long time to shed. She was dark and pretty, and the fact that Russell Means was a handsome dude in his younger days said something about her beauty, as he had his pick of women at the time. The Weltanschauung of the movement meant, among other things, that a woman might be with one man one day and a couple of days later be seen with someone else. The cowgirl later wrote, asking if I wanted to come to South Dakota. I did, but my little girl was only two years old and I couldn't leave her.

On our return trip to Montana, some of us stopped along the way; the other two cars of university students went ahead. We were lolly-gagging because a couple of our men had women from South Dakota reservations with them. We went to the Sisseton reservation and par-tied all night in a bar known as the Pool Hall. As closing time came, the bartender – a fairly young half-blood guy – locked the doors from the inside and continued to sell us drinks. When a quarrel broke out over a woman, the bartender drew a shotgun from under the bar and shot through the men's bathroom door to quiet the argument. I had just come from the bathroom about a minute before the shotgun pellets tore through its door; it's lucky no one was in the bathroom at the time, as the latrine was directly in the line of fire. After we ran out of cigarettes, the bartender walked to the coin-operated cigarette machine, smashed the glass, and told the smokers, "I'll just tell the boss AIM was in here and they did it." We had cigarettes and, in our drunken state, readily accepted his blame of the movement – hell, we had just occupied a federal building, what was a cigarette machine?

Reclaiming

12

It took us about ten days to return to Missoula, delayed by partying and womanizing. We arrived shortly before the Thanksgiving holiday, which was a loaded occasion for white Americans and Indians. We cast about for something symbolic upon which to act in conjunction with the holiday. On the east side of Missoula, a large wooden Indian stood chained to the cinder block column that supported a carport outside the registration office of a motel.

I thought of the statue as Kaw-liga, a wooden Indian that was the subject of a popular 1950s country-and-western song sung by Hank Williams Sr. The lyrics of that song are highly racist. Kaw-liga is in love with an Indian maid in an antique store but is so backward and stupid that he doesn't know how to tell her he loves her. One day a wealthy (white) customer comes into the shop and buys the Indian maid.

Somebody made good money in this country carving wooden Indians; they graced many tobacco shops at one time. A cigar store Indian, unlike the real ones, is a good Indian – good because he just sits still and takes it. He's so stoic anyone can just walk on up and take the woman he's in love with. Ask Hank Williams. Some wag, back in the inventiveness of the hippie era, made a poster featuring the Indian image on the Indian-head nickel and a logo: THE ONLY INDIAN AMERICA EVER LOVED. I've always thought that was apropos.

We decided to rescue the wooden Indian. Dennis Decoteau, a revolutionary genius for subverting white kind of thinking into something we could use, proposed to write a press release to the local daily newspaper, the *Missoulian*, explaining that the wooden Indian, chained to the post, represented the American Indian who was in chains to white greed and chicanery. A woman we knew who had been let in on our plans agreed to let us stow the wooden Indian under her trailer house.

In the late afternoon of Thanksgiving Day, as the rest of America settled down for their sumptuous turkey dinners, four of us cruised the streets of Missoula, working up our courage to liberate Kaw-liga. Certainly the motel registration clerk would see us as we got out of the car and, with a pair of bolt cutters, cut the chained and aggrieved Indian loose from his bondage, load him into the car, and speed off.

We decided to wait until dark. Like stealing horses from an Assiniboine camp, it would be more effectively done with darkness an added ally. We also considered the possibility of getting shot by the motel clerk. Americans and the tenets of American law would no doubt acclaim the death of a wooden-Indian thief justifiable homicide.

Pulling up to Kaw-liga about eight that evening, we quickly went to work on the chain, cutting it with the bolt cutter. We then leaned our wooden, long-suffering brother over to stuff him into the back seat. Alas, neither rear door could be shut – we hadn't counted on his height.

With our strange and silent passenger sticking out both rear doors of the car and held down by two back seat passengers, we sped away onto dark residential streets. We drove carefully; it was an old part of Missoula and the streets were narrow, forcing us to slow down and move to the right as cars passed in the opposite direction to prevent them from cutting off Kaw-liga's feet. After hiding him under the woman's trailer house, we sent a typed press release to the *Missoulian* explaining the reason for the action and pointing out the hypocrisy of Thanksgiving Day in the land of the free and the brave.

Our long-term plan was to keep the wooden Indian secreted until the big university powwow in April and then bring him out during the forty-nine, which would follow in Pattee Canyon, a short distance up in the mountains. We would bring Kaw-liga to the forty-nine, introduce him around, and then set him aflame. That plan was aborted and replaced by a better one. During the subsequent Wounded Knee occupation, my cousin George Kipp and others took Kaw-liga to a highly visible spot in Missoula, doused him with gas, and set him afire. Harley Hettick, at that time the staff photographer for the *Missoulian*, photographed the event and then blew the picture up to poster size.

I returned to the University of Montana a different kind of a student than when I had left. By taking political science classes effectively first-hand, I more clearly understood how my people came to be in their present condition and I saw for myself the reaction of whites when confronted with the political reality of the treaty issue.

We who had traveled by caravan to Washington DC became minor celebrities and were asked to speak to civic groups and classes at the university. Even then, many of us still believed in the junior high rhetoric of equality for all. The sentiment was difficult to get rid of, as it was buried so deep and sounded so good; even today it sounds good, though it isn't true. After the BIA building occupation, I spoke to a grade school class at the invitation of a white woman teacher. When I asked the grade school students if they knew anything about what had happened in DC, one boy replied his dad had said they should bomb the Indians back to the stone age. We are not born equal, and real political equality was not meant for anyone but the white male. At the beginning of the twenty-first century, some change in inequality is taking place. Some. Not a whole lot.

I was soon visited by the FBI. They came at least a couple of times, seeking information about the whereabouts of the documents removed from the BIA building when the occupation ended. Those records, containing evidence of fraud, became the basis of columns by the widely read writer Jack Anderson. People, including Anderson, would face subpoenas as to the whereabouts of the records. I knew that records had been taken but did not know who had them. Once the information started leaking out about what had been uncovered in the documents, it made the trip seem worthwhile.

Though I didn't tell Jean about the Sisseton cowgirl, she must have sensed something. We argued several times after I returned. One night after staying out late with some of the AIM members at a bar, I came home to find all my clothes on the front lawn. I picked up my clothes and headed for the railroad tracks in Missoula, on the north side of town, where stood a cluster of tiny shacks that could be rented for twenty-two dollars a month. Although known as the Wine Shacks, in the fall of 1972, hippies, dope dealers, and other low-end types were also living there. I stayed there and continued school, as did Jean.

One day Sherman Jenkins, a friend of mine from a Wyoming tribe and married to a cousin of mine, showed up at the Wine Shacks. Earlier that week he also had been kicked out by his wife, so he brought some of his clothes, including his guitar, to my place. Sherman was ebullient as it was his birthday and he had already begun celebrating. He invited me to go with him to Eddie's Club, a local hippie hangout. We felt a certain comfort with the hippies, as they were also outcasts from society and rebellious. Other taverns would moan when a bunch of Indians invaded their joint. Indian money spent as well as anyone else's, but bartenders and bar owners had come to know that when Indians get drunk they don't just act silly, they become mouthy and mean and are prone to fight and break hell out of good bar furniture. The hippies, in their own journeys away from their American roots, had read *Black Elk Speaks*, had grown their hair long, just like the Hopi prophecy said they would, and had a name similar to the Hopi, which the prophecy also said would come to be. We thus shared a kind of arms-length kinship with the longhaired, misbegotten children of the American Dream.

Sherman had some money. Indians can be broke when the phone

bill arrives, but they somehow always seem to come up with money when it's time to drink. Leon Rattler, an artist and educator, once told me his grandmother, castigating him for drinking, told him that he would always have money to drink on, that the Devil would always provide the wherewithal to make sure his soul was on the highway to nowhere. It sure seems that way. On that day, we drank shots of tequila to celebrate Sherman's birthday, chasing the shots with gulps of draft beer. We learned of a party that was going to take place that evening at a house of a friend.

We decided about six that evening to first retrieve Sherman's guitar at my shack before going to the party. We were feeling pretty robust, having been in the bar since about two. When we arrived at the Wine Shacks, Sherman went to use the bathroom, a shack used in common by the renters. Just as he reached for the door to the bathroom, it sprung open and hit him in the face. On a normal day this probably would not have happened, because Sherman would most likely have been alert enough to see the door as it started to open. But this day was his birthday, and we had just consumed about a fifth of tequila and a gallon of beer between us. His eyes were a little glazed and a rollin' in the sockets. Hearing loud, angry voices, I peered out the door of my Wine Shack and spied Sherman arguing with one of the local hippie drug dealers over being smacked between the eyes with the toilet door. I went out to join in the debate. Drunks always think they are great mediators, think that conflict resolution is right down their foggy alley.

The loud exchange attracted other young white hippies from the Wine Shack of the drug dealer. They had apparently been drinking and probably doping. When I reached the altercation, one of the drug dealer's friends looked at me.

"What's the matter?" I asked.

The young white guy shot back, "None of your fucking business."

The tequila in full bloom, without even replying, I hit him in the mouth, and the fight was on. Soon a couple more guys joined in, and Sherman and I were badly outnumbered. I was knocked down into a pile of firewood, two-by-four scraps from local lumber mills stacked about ten feet high in front of the Wine Shacks. Three white guys pummeling me, I managed to scramble higher onto the pile of two-by-four pieces. I then grabbed a block of wood and hurled it at the head of a tormentor coming up the woodpile. This sudden supply of ammunition gave me that moment of clarity one needs in a dire situation – I was over the top of the woodpile and gone. It was a cowardly act, leaving my partner in the middle of a fight, but the survival instinct was stronger. Bolting between two of the Wine Shacks, I came across another ample supply of ammunition. The big red rocks lining the railroad bed were just about the right size to throw; as the first of my adversaries came through the space between the buildings, I pelted him hard enough to turn him. His partners, seeing the rock supply I was standing on, cussed me out and disappeared. At about the same time I saw Sherman emerge forty yards away. By the time we arrived at the party, our bruises were apparent. I had a fat lip and other bruises here and there, and Sherman had a black eye and bruises. We had discovered that hippies might talk peace, but it was just a decoy, that they were as violent as their forebears.[1]

Some of the AIM warriors at the party that evening were incensed that we had been thumped by hippies. As the party wore on, a couple of them vowed revenge, and after a bit the momentum gathered for a revenge raid, a time-honored Blackfeet tradition. When the enemy strikes a blow and hurts you, it's time to regroup, sally forth, and pay him back double, triple, quadruple – make him cry. That was an old Blackfeet prayer as they called upon their ancestor warrior sprits for aid in warfare – help me make the enemy cry.

A carload of people, with me as guide, wound our way through the streets of Missoula to the Wine Shacks. There were five or six men and three or four women in our group, some of the young men from the Kicking Horse Job Corps Center, and a couple of my cousins. We parked and approached the shack of the dope dealer, but the lights were out; hippies, after getting good and stoned, often sat with only a candle lit. We crept up and peeked in the window, but it was curtained. Someone tried the door, but it was locked. A hard kick broke the lock open, and in we poured; I hung back as I'd already taken one beating that day and didn't care for another. Nobody was there, so we trashed the place. Another dope dealer who lived about three doors down heard the commotion and came out of his Wine Shack. When our group saw a white man shouting at us, wanting to know what in the hell we were doing trashing his friend's Wine Shack, my cronies mistook him for one of the hippies we were seeking. I knew he hadn't been in the fight that afternoon, but they overpowered him before I could set the record straight. The Indians gave the dope dealer a good whacking, the same kind I had received that afternoon – the odds uneven, hitting him over the head with a two-by-four piece of firewood. When his girlfriend and a friend of hers in his shack started screaming, they were severely thrashed by the women with us. Then we left.

It was decided as the party broke up later that it might not be safe for me to sleep alone, so at 5:00 a.m. about five AIM warriors came with me and slept on the floor. At about ten that morning a vigorous pounding on the door woke us. Were we in for another battle? Peering out the window next to the door, I saw a white guy who lived in a corner Wine Shack and who, as far as I was concerned, was a pretty fair dude, having visited with him a couple of times. I opened the door. The white man told me we'd better get out, as he had heard the hippies talking late last night when they had returned to find their shack turned upside down. They were looking for a shotgun to blow the fuckin' Indians to Kingdom Come. The days of living peacefully among the flower children were over. We armed ourselves. I moved out that day while my brothers stood guard, but fortunately for everyone, the hippies with the shotgun never appeared.

Jean (pregnant again) and I reconciled, and in January of 1973 I returned to classes at the University of Montana. It was a time of escalating tensions between Indian activists and the federal government. AIM issued a call, and some of the Missoula Blackfeet AIM members, the single ones like G.G. Kipp (Eagle Flag), Buzz Heavy Runner, and Bradley LaPlant, went to fight in Rapid City. Other Blackfeet, including Charles "Buzz" Momberg, Leon Rattler, and Stormy Bear Child, joined them there.

During this time of growing turbulence, our lives went on. Jean and I were expecting our second child around the twentieth of February. I was studying journalism and taking some creative writing classes. I took a class with the great University of Montana poet Richard Hugo and thoroughly enjoyed it; nobody in my family had ever hinted at an affinity with poetry.

Through phone contact with AIM warriors and television reports, I was aware of the deepening conflict. On February 6, 1973, a violent confrontation took place at the Custer Courthouse in South Dakota. It seems that an Oglala man, Wesley Bad Heart Bull, had been murdered in Buffalo Gap, South Dakota, but the accused had been charged only with manslaughter. Around 200 AIM members and supporters protested and rioted.

Jean went to the hospital to have our baby, and our daughter Dameon was born on the momentous evening of February 27, at about the same time that Russell Means and Dennis Banks led 250 AIM members, supporters, and Oglalas who were opposed to the Pine Ridge Lakota tribal council to a hamlet on the Pine Ridge reservation called Wounded Knee. The siege had begun.

Defending   13

For ten weeks, AIM and some supporters occupied the small town of Wounded Knee, South Dakota, the site of the infamous massacre of hundreds of Lakotas in December 1890. AIM leaders Russell Means, Clyde Belcourt, and Dennis Banks received the attention of the national media and played important roles during the occupation; spiritual leaders like Leonard Crow Dog and Frank Fools Crow, the ancient Sun Dance leader, were also present.

At the start of the occupation, AIM alerted all its chapters that it needed manpower and supplies. Many responded. Wounded Knee appealed to Indian people at different levels. Aside from the activists in college, some Indians who lived on the streets, lives filled with alcohol and dysfunction, were quick to recognize the merits of the movement. Perhaps they could not articulate the reasons socially and politically, but they knew something was fundamentally wrong with life on the reservation. Many didn't have jobs, so taking part in protests was a step up from panhandling for drinks on the streets.

I convinced my journalism professor at the university that the occupation was worth attending as a journalism student, and he agreed. My other professors also thought it was a historic occasion, so I made arrangements to make up their classes or do a report on the occupation when I returned. I saw my baby girl and Jean for a few hours, purchased a snub-nosed .38, and went to pick up Bradley LaPlant at

Al's Bar, another rough place where Indians hung out in Missoula. Newly returned from Rapid City, behind in his classes, and having fallen in love with a woman who would become his wife, my cousin G.G. decided to stay behind in Missoula. Accompanying us was Joe Boy Morris, who had been living a hard life. He had been drinking heavily at Al's Bar but insisted that he wanted to go to Wounded Knee. Though I didn't know Joe Boy, we let him ride with us. He was Blackfeet. He was family.

I funded our trip, having received some lease money from land the BIA administered on the Blackfeet reservation. I had been saving the BIA check for some time for another purpose but cashed it so we would have money to go to Wounded Knee. As a university student, Bradley only had a little money in his pocket, about forty dollars. Joe Boy had no money, having been homeless on the streets of Missoula. Unfortunately, I lost my money and main set of keys somewhere on the way to South Dakota, along with my wallet. We had stopped in a rough bar in Billings, where I wasn't careful enough watching my jacket when I went to the bathroom. I didn't realize the loss until we were ready to continue our journey and couldn't find my keys to open the car door. Luckily, I did carry a spare ignition key.

Listening to the radio reports as we left Billings in my Pontiac and headed down I-90 to Pine Ridge, we learned that the FBI and the U.S. Marshals had cordoned off the Wounded Knee area. We had sipped some beer between Missoula and Billings but soon abstained because of the growing seriousness of the matter. Approaching the Pine Ridge reservation, we weren't sure how to reach Wounded Knee with the roads blocked. In the middle of the night we decided to rest and continue at daylight. In the Black Hills, not too far from Custer, South Dakota, the scene of the recent AIM riot, we pulled off the highway, parked in a hayfield, and attempted to go to sleep. A pair of headlights suddenly appeared, approaching us.

A white man behind the glare of headlights shouted at us. "What are you doing in my hayfield?"

Rolling the window down, I yelled back, "We're going to take a rest, we're traveling, we're tired."

He wouldn't have it. "You can't stay there," he retorted. This was the white mind at work, the owning mind, the lost mind, the mind that nobody, not even a large portion of his own womenfolk, really understood. It is a clever mechanical mind, no doubt about that. But it is a mind that thinks it owns the world, and one day the world – maybe sooner than later – is going to prove matters otherwise. Maybe the reason white people are so jumpy about their "property" is the hidden guilt over the theft of the land, a guilt that keeps them from feeling settled, from allowing them as sentient human beings to view the land. Instead, they are like trolls with guns.

Peeking from the backseat and increasingly paranoid due to heavy drinking, Joe Boy claimed the white guy was holding a gun. We couldn't see the man; his headlights shone in our eyes. Most ranchers are violent and carry guns, living out the American dream of conquest. So, we left the hayfield.

Having been through Pine Ridge on the Trail of Broken Treaties, I remembered somewhat how the road from Oelrich came into Pine Ridge, so we traveled down Highway 18 for a distance. Now on the Pine Ridge reservation, we pulled off onto a side road and into a bare field to sleep. Quite certainly an Indian wouldn't kick us out of a field simply for resting there.

A couple of hours of sleep under our belts, we drove through Pine Ridge Village the next morning. About a hundred federal marshals stood across from the BIA building, and people scurried to and fro. The tension was palpable. Not knowing anybody in Pine Ridge to whom we might ask assistance in getting to Wounded Knee, we decided to call an AIM number in Rapid City that had been provided for those who wanted to take part in the occupation. We phoned from a bar in White Clay, Nebraska, and were told that people would be taken into Wounded Knee from a home in Rapid City later that day.

In a hurry to get to Rapid City, we stopped in Oelrich for gas. We had already spent some of Bradley's money on food, so after filling the Pontiac's gas tank, thirteen dollars and some cents remained. Several white guys were loitering at the gas station when I went in to pay. Longhaired Indians were new and suspected AIM members, so as soon as I – wild looking with long, unkempt hair – stepped through the door, the bad air, the hostility, rolled toward me. Those cowboys and farmers, who probably leased reservation land, most likely had been talking about the takeover at Wounded Knee, now in its third day and the big news on nightly television. I noticed that the pickups in the parking lot had rifles in the rear windows, standard fare for cattle country. The cowboys and farmers had to keep the coyote population in check, and now they were probably wondering if they weren't going to be called upon to keep the longhaired radical Indian population in check.

What those cowboys and farmers didn't know was that I knew them much better than they knew me. Once in the car, I warned Bradley about the cowboys. He agreed to be careful, declaring that it wouldn't be above rednecks like that to pull alongside us and shoot through the window.

Bradley now drove. He didn't have a driver's license, but mine was lost. I'm not sure Joe Boy even knew how to drive; he always walked around the Blackfeet reservation. Our withdrawal from alcohol had put Joe Boy in a bad way. The night before he had been talking to himself and, when asked, said he was speaking to the dead. We were leery of him, as we thought he might go into DTS.

About four or five miles after the gas station, Bradley pushed the big Pontiac up to about eighty, and suddenly there was a loud explosion as a rear tire blew out. Joe Boy, his nerves without alcohol flagellating against the powers of sobriety, screamed and dove to the floor in the back. He was convinced that the rednecks had caught us and were shooting. A pitiful and serious predicament, but Bradley and I couldn't contain ourselves and burst out laughing at Joe Boy's combat readiness.

Our laughter didn't last long. We couldn't get into the trunk to change the tire without my lost key ring. After a few minutes, a pickup truck carrying two white men came into view, going in our direction. I hailed the truck down. The man on the passenger side rolled the window down cautiously – not much, about two inches, but enough for me to speak to them. I asked the driver if we could borrow a bar of some kind, a tire iron or something similar with which to pry the trunk open. Although a tire iron was clearly visible in the back of their truck, the driver refused my request and said that they would return to the service station and send someone out to help us.

They were afraid. I had grown up among white people, but those two men hadn't grown up among Indians. Though they might have lived in proximity to the Pine Ridge Indian reservation, they probably had very little contact with Indians on a personal basis. Their views were presumably shaped by the violent attitudes promoted in western movies and the stories told in their families of battles their great-grandfathers had had with Indians while taking Indian land. The news reports of armed Indians occupying Wounded Knee must have escalated their mistrust and the fear of all Indians. They weren't totally wrong.

"Fucking pricks, they didn't want to help us," I told Bradley as they left.

Admittedly, we looked pretty rough. Bradley and I were both growing our hair out, and anybody with hair over his shirt collar looks scruffy. At that length, there's nothing to be done, as it can't be put into anything resembling order; it's too short to braid and too short for a ponytail, so you just have to let it fall where it may. It is also probable that the two white men saw my car as too nice for Indians to own or drive. Most of the Pine Ridge Lakota people drove old cars – second- or third-hand cars that smoked, broke, balked, and didn't cost much. Something was amiss in this picture for the two white men in the pickup truck. The Indians didn't have the trunk key for such a glossy piece of American industrial ingenuity. Why didn't they have the key? They probably stole the car and its (white) owner is lying in a ditch somewhere.

One thing you learn growing up on the prairie is that you can't afford to be helpless; you have to learn to improvise. We pulled a metal post out of a fence running alongside the highway, stuck it under the lip of the trunk, and, with all three of us prying upward, managed to spring the trunk lock. We changed the tire and put the fence post back in the ground.

In the meantime, the white men in the truck had apparently called the highway patrol. Before we had traveled two miles, a highway patrol car came at high speed from the opposite direction. Approaching us he slowed and, in the instant we passed him, swung the patrol car around and turned on his siren and lights. None of us had licenses, so we were forced to follow him into the town of Hot Springs and be taken before a judge. After an hour wait in an anteroom, we were ushered in before a judge, and we pleaded guilty to driving without licenses. The resulting fine was about fifty dollars more than what we had in our possession. We told him we only had thirteen dollars and some odd cents.

The judge thought deeply for a moment and said, "Well, boys, I'll tell you what. I just came from church, that's why you had to wait for me, and I'm feeling pretty good after going to church. So give me your thirteen dollars, and that will take care of it."

One might say the Great Spirit intervened on our behalf. We walked out and were soon on our way to Rapid City. We were free but broke.

OWMT (Old White Man Trick): Pick you up for breaking one of his laws, take your money, and turn you loose so you can restart the cycle.

OIT (Old Indian Trick): We never have much money to take.

In Rapid City, we again called the AIM number from a pay phone and gave them our location; they said to stay at the phone for a few minutes. We thought they were going to call us back, but soon an Indian guy showed up, having driven by and checked us out to make sure we were skins before approaching.

We joined several carloads of Indians at Muriel Waukazoo's house in Rapid City. Late that afternoon, in caravan fashion, we started for Porcupine, as Wounded Knee could not now be reached by car. We traveled back roads, since it was feared the feds would attempt to stop us on the main highways. That evening we pulled off a gravel road some dozen miles from Wounded Knee. We would walk in later. A short distance away sat a small frame house, the home of Severt Young Bear. Indians, many with guns, were sitting inside the house, milling around outside, and coming and going. They fed us, and we went and sat outside and listened to the talk of those who knew what was happening inside Wounded Knee. Although reports of military "tanks" being unloaded at Pine Ridge were not quite accurate – armored personnel carriers were actually being unloaded – the idea of heavy military equipment being brought to the siege gave the occupation a new dimension of gravity. A cold, sleety rain began to fall that evening.

Joe Boy, coming off the sauce, was in tough shape. As there was no place to sleep in the crowded house, we slept in my Pontiac, I in the front seat and Bradley and Joe Boy in back. Sometime in the early morning darkness, I woke to Bradley castigating Joe Boy, telling him to shut up and go back to sleep. Joe Boy continued whispering to himself, saying that tanks were coming. The sound of gravel being kicked up by cars on the road a couple hundred yards away was easily heard, and Joe Boy, in his near-DT condition, apparently thought the vehicles were tanks.

It was still raining, miserably cold, when we crawled out of the car in the morning. By that time Joe Boy was fully paranoid, convinced that the Indians walking around with rifles, pistols, and shotguns believed him an informer and were going to kill him. (I'm not sure where he got the idea of being an informer, which, after Wounded Knee, would become a central issue and cause great disruption within the ranks of AIM.) All of a sudden, Joe Boy did not want to be there. Some of the people in charge said to take him to a church located a quarter mile off the road and deliver him to the preacher. They said they knew the preacher and the man of the cloth would take care of him. We loaded Joe Boy into the backseat and took him to the church. The rain, however, made it impossible to get off the gravel road without getting stuck in the muddy dirt road that led to the church. Joe Boy wasn't deterred; he got out and took off for the church at a dead run. I wouldn't see him again for several years, not until he came back to the Blackfeet reservation from the West Coast, where he had been living.

An old Lakota man, Douglas Horse, and his wife lived a short distance from Severt Young Bear's house and invited several of us to come to their house for a meal that afternoon. That is a code of the traditional people – they always feed you. We ate bannock bread, rice, and some boiled meat. In the trunk of my car, I had an oversized frying pan that I used for camping, and later I went to the old lady and gave her the frying pan for feeding us.[1]

Sometime later, Bradley and I were sitting in my car when a woman approached and knocked on the window. When I rolled the window down, Cordelia Attack Him asked if I was interested in going to a Yuwipi ceremony that evening. I had smoked the Sacred Pipe at Mount Rushmore the previous year but had never been to a Yuwipi ceremony, a spirit calling ceremony. I had heard Indian people talk about it, and I didn't doubt for one minute that a man could call spirits into a ceremony – my sister Katherine was constantly seeing and hearing spirits without even trying, and I had grown up fearfully believing in spirits, ghosts, and unearthly beings who could manifest. Despite my trepidation, I told Cordelia Attack Him that I was interested in attending the ceremony. She gave me directions on how to get to her home and said I could follow her to the ceremony from there. Bradley declined to attend, admitting that he had never been in a ceremony of that sort and the strangeness of it was a bit overwhelming.[2]

That evening we drove to the home of John and Cordelia Attack Him. I accompanied them to the ceremony, while Bradley stayed behind at their house. Soon we were sitting in the living room of a frame house on the outskirts of Porcupine. All the furniture had been removed; people sat on blankets with their backs against the wall. The conversation was casual, joking. When the ceremonial leader or doctor, Alphonse Good Shield, entered, the energy changed as he began setting up his altar for the ceremony, stringing the tobacco ties and putting his four flags of cloth – red, black, white, and yellow – in coffee cans that now held dirt. Men who had entered with the ceremonial leader took hand drums from cloth sacks, went into the kitchen, turned on the electric stove, and warmed the drumheads over the burners.

Cordelia explained that once the ceremony started, Alphonse Good Shield could not speak English. Although he was Cordelia's brother, in his role of calling the spirit messengers of the Great Mystery to the little frame house in which we sat, he was also a brother to all of us. This wasn't my perception of religion. There were spirits and another layer of reality, I was sure. The spirit world had never been presented to me in such a detailed, logical, and moral framework, however.

With all in readiness, the lights in the little frame house were turned off. The windows had been covered from the inside with blankets tacked snugly against them; there wasn't an iota of light to be seen anywhere. You could put your hand in front of your nose and not be able to see it. As the old cowman said, "It was darker than the inside of a cow." Dark upon dark.

I jumped about six inches into the air when one of the singers suddenly hit his drum. The other three drummers also began pounding their drums in unison and soon began to sing. Indian singing of course wasn't new to me. My pop, you will recall, sang Indian every evening at home while playing solitaire. This Yuwipi singing, accompanied by drums, signified something going on at a deeper level, something you couldn't put on paper, something people refer to as that still small voice, the subconscious, the conscience, the untapped part of the gray matter.

Something started to come into focus in the light-spilling atmosphere of that total darkness. One of the infinite arms of God was preparing to reach into that small, hot room, which was throbbing with hide-covered drums. Miles away, white men cussed their luck at having been chosen for duty far from the glitz of America, not knowing there was something as holy as their Christ parting the molecules of the South Dakota air that night. The Holy Ghost was coming.

Some of the people in attendance had come for physical healing. The medicine man, now limited to speaking Lakota, told his sister what had been said by the beings from the other side. A strange concept, I thought, communicating with beings from the other side. Christian theologians didn't relish discussing such an idea. Until this ceremony I didn't know that medicine men in the Indian way talk to the other side. I had uncovered another part of what the various churches, mainly the Catholic Church, had hidden.

During Good Shield's ceremony he translated to Cordelia that he had just traveled to Wounded Knee and that at that moment a ceremony was also taking place there, conducted by Crow Dog. I was without a point of reference. What does he mean he's going into Wounded Knee? Are we to sit here and wait for him to walk into Wounded Knee and then come back? The Catholic Church hadn't taught me that men can travel astrally, that their spirits, their consciousness, their energy, can leave the body and go places. I sat in total darkness, wondering how in hell this guy was going into Wounded Knee. His drummers started drumming and singing; in a few minutes they quit and the man spoke. His sister said that he had just visited Wounded Knee and that three men were walking out, that he had passed them. I was pretty skeptical when I heard this – yeah, well, anybody could say they did that. The ceremony continued a while longer, ended, and then the usual traditional feed was held for all the participants. The food reflected the conditions of the Indians present – big red wieners, boiled potatoes, cookies, and coffee.

We returned to Johnny Attack Him's house, where we had been invited to spend the night; because he was Cordelia's brother, the medicine man Good Shield would also be staying there. I was curious about what I had experienced and was interested in hearing what he had to say. We talked, however, mainly about other matters; John and the medicine man spoke about local issues, some associated with the ongoing occupation.

Cordelia was in the kitchen making coffee when suddenly she called for her husband in an urgent voice. He rose and strode toward the kitchen. In a moment we heard a shout and rose together to see what was happening. When we reached the kitchen, John Attack Him was just stepping out the door into the night. We followed, and John whispered to Alphonse Good Shield that someone was hollering from the hillside in front of us. Again John Attack Him shouted and, again, a response. We stood for a few moments looking toward the dark hillside. Then, three figures emerged out of the darkness.

Immediately my mind raced to what Good Shield had said in the ceremony: three men were walking out of Wounded Knee. Those men – Herb Powless, Ron Poteet, and Ted Means – said they had indeed come from the besieged village. So it *was* possible for a man to travel outside his body; it was possible for his spirit to leave his physical body, go somewhere, and come back. That particular moment, that ingestion of knowledge proved to be a turning point for me.

The following evening just after dark, thirty-nine of us started to walk into Wounded Knee guided by two Native teenage boys. We had three horses that were loaded with gunnysacks containing a variety of goods, primarily food, much of it government surplus food that the locals had donated. It was chilly but not bitterly cold, probably a few degrees above freezing, and about two crunchy inches of snow covered the ground as we walked. The march went well enough for ten or so miles until we were about two miles from Wounded Knee. At that point, one young Indian woman, a Flathead from Montana who was fatigued from walking in the snow, started to sit down, complaining she couldn't go any farther. A couple of the other women began cursing and trying to get her to her feet. Finally, we decided the Flathead woman could ride on one of the horses.

She had only ridden for about a half mile when an engine suddenly roared and a bright light lit up a hillside a quarter of a mile from where we stood. When the armored personnel carrier crawled toward us with its bright spotlight scanning the landscape, we ducked down into a nearby ravine. We decided quickly that it would be too risky to take the horses farther; on foot we could dodge in the darkness, but the horses would be too vulnerable, too large a target in the glare of the APC spotlight. People took food from the sacks and put it into their shirts and coat pockets. I loaded into my military style pack a large amount of ammunition people had donated, mostly cartridges for deer hunting rifles and some shotgun shells. The Flathead woman who had been riding could only be coaxed from the horse when someone observed that the APC had a machine gun as well as a searchlight and that she would become a mighty big target if the APC caught the horse in the light. We led the three horses back to the head of the coulee, unsaddled them and hid the saddles in some willow brush, and then turned them loose. The horses started home the way we had come.

It now seemed as if our footsteps could be heard for a long distance on the crunchy snow. The APC had crawled over the top of a hill not too far away and parked with its searchlight fanning out and shining toward Wounded Knee, the direction we wanted to go. At the moment, we were safe deep within the willow bottom of the coulee, crouching down, waiting to see which way the APC went.

Suddenly a popping sound punctuated the night. I was shocked – I *knew* that sound. I had heard it every night for twenty months in Vietnam as the security forces defended the air base at Da Nang, unleashing flares to light up the Vietnamese night to see if Victor Charlie was coming through the concertina wire. In that moment in the ravine, I realized the United States military was looking for *me* with those flares. *I was the gook now.* No wonder the Vietnamese, looking at the Indian tattoo on my arm, had presciently told me, *You same same Viet Cong.* I damn sure was. Right here in good old America, the land of the democratic tradition, the home of the free, the brave, yes, in my own homeland, the one I had eagerly sallied forth to defend some seven years previously, the home of Kentucky Fried, Buicks, and blonde beauties, home to the Declaration of Independence that my seventh grade mind believed, home to the Constitution that said the treaties we signed were instruments of international law, that country, that one, was now sending up a flare in the night, a bright popping flare that was looking for *me*. The previous night I had experienced an epiphany when I realized a man could travel out of his body; now, one night later, I underwent another one as I realized this country was not what I thought it was. Two major veils had been rent.

We waited out of sight until the roar of the APC was distant and then, moving down the ravine and out onto the prairie, began trudging the final couple of miles to Wounded Knee. About a mile from the hamlet, we heard a big bass Indian drum sending its reverberations into the frosty night air. The music was satisfying to us but probably frightening to the white men in the APCs. Through their own stories, their own media, they have created an inordinate fear of savages pounding a tom-tom. But in their rush upon the land to claim it, they never took time to find out what things of this land meant. Some, like the drum, have been here a long time and have a very deep metaphysical meaning, not only for Natives but anyone who travels the land. The drum says this: the sound you hear is the sound of the universe, the sound of the heart of God beating, breathing energy into your own heart; it is the sound of the collective heart of all mankind, beating in rhythm, in unison, telling us we all come from the source that created that heartbeat.

Following that deeply resonant drumbeat, we reached the Wounded Knee village sometime in the wee hours of the morning, maybe three or four o'clock, and were greeted enthusiastically by those occupiers still awake at that far hour. An old lady named Sally was sitting with some younger people in the basement of the Catholic church, and one thing she said as we were fed stew has always remained in my mind. A young woman from our group, surprised at the age of the elderly woman, who was in her eighties, asked her why she was taking part in the occupation. The old lady jerked her thumb over her shoulder. In the direction she jerked her thumb was the mass grave of those Lakotas killed in the Wounded Knee massacre of 1890. The Catholic church in which we sat (and which later burned down) stood directly in front of the mass grave. "I have a lot of my people buried out there," she replied, simply.

We slept in the attic of the church and the next day went out and looked around. Bunkers had been constructed here and there on the perimeter and were being manned by mainly young Indian men and women. A couple of vehicles were being used for running chores. At a security meeting, Bradley and I, both Vietnam veterans, were assigned a bunker. Our bunker sat on a hillside and was called the Denby Bunker. We commandeered a small trailer about forty yards behind the bunker that had been abandoned by a white construction worker at the time of the occupation. It was very small, about fifteen feet long with a kitchen area on one end, a table in the middle, and a bedroom at the other end. It served to get us out of the chilly wind when we weren't on bunker duty, watching the feds. We could see the APCs about a half mile out; they in turn had parked so they could watch us. Unfortunately, I was armed only with my snub-nosed Saturday Night Special; the war would have to be up close and personal before I could effectively defend Wounded Knee.

Like Vietnam, like the occupation of the BIA building, like all wars, periods of intense boredom were only occasionally shattered by moments of intense adrenalin. On the second day came a report of a firefight. We saw a van with Indians speeding over the bridge a short distance away, and soon the van raced back. We found out later that someone, a man named Poor Bear if I recall correctly, had been shot in the hand. After five days we heard that the government was imposing an ultimatum: by the following evening we were to lay down our weapons and surrender. Throughout the next day a feeling of unease grew as the deadline neared. In the afternoon word was sent that we were to leave at least one man in each bunker while the rest of the warriors were to gather in a tipi set up directly under the hill where the mass grave was located. Leonard Crow Dog, the medicine man, was going to do a sweat lodge and paint the faces of the warriors for battle, for death if need be. Bradley and I left a couple of other men at the bunker and went to the tipi. The sweat lodge in process, we waited outside for Crow Dog to emerge. Neither Bradley nor I had ever been in a sweat lodge.

Journalists from around the world had by that time converged on Wounded Knee. Some had been in the hamlet before the government shut down access; others attempted to gather news from the surrounding environs, including the BIA offices and the tribal council offices. By the time we went to the tipi to be painted by Crow Dog for the showdown, some foreign journalists had gathered there, presumably similarly guided into Wounded Knee under cover of darkness.

For those not familiar with how a sweat lodge runs, there are normally four rounds, between which the covering on the sweat lodge door is opened to give the sweating and praying people inside some fresh air and a brief respite from the intense heat. On that night a handful of journalists gathered outside the sweat lodge, waiting, as we were, for the ceremony to conclude. They had been instructed not to take pictures of the ceremony, but at least some undoubtedly would write about what they saw later. As the door of the sweat lodge opened at one point, some of the journalists, including a very attractive young woman, of possibly French or Italian origin, crowded around the opening to see what it looked like inside. As she peered into the darkness of the sweat lodge, her colleagues, also trying to see inside, accidentally shoved the woman journalist. She fell forward into the entrance of the lodge. As it was a traditional warrior sweat lodge, all the participants were male and totally nude; right inside the door was a man with his feet pulled up against his body so that his large dangling testicles could be seen from where I stood a few feet behind the journalists. As the woman journalist fell, she turned sideways to protect her camera around her neck and ended up face to face with large pieces of manhood a few inches from her curious nose. Needless to say, she extricated herself from that gaggle of newshounds in a hurry, not a little surprised and embarrassed from her brief sojourn into the mysteries of a Native sweat lodge.

The ceremony finished, Crow Dog emerged, and we went into the tipi, which contained a buffalo skull altar where we knelt to pray while he painted our faces for war and possibly death. If we died on that day, we wanted to leave showing the Creator that we were one of his children, which is what the paint, in that particular context, meant. We returned to our bunker to await whatever fate was ours.

When the deadline arrived at six that evening, the APCs stayed in place. In the hour following the deadline we were informed that the government had extended the deadline for another day. The next day was also tense and full of anticipation, but at the end of that day another deadline was given.

Sometime about the third or fourth day after the initial deadline, I went to the Catholic church to get something to eat. I helped others unload food that had been brought in; supplies were damn scarce. A kind of slumgummy stew had been the prevailing fuel in the past few days. One of the white ranchers had cattle that had roamed a little too close to the Wounded Knee perimeter, and they were herded in for sustenance. I happened to get some rice soup that had been made with one of the bulls, an unintentional donation. Real good choppers and strong jaws were needed to chew that bull meat.

I had struck up a flirting friendship with a very pretty woman from Sisseton; women from that reservation seemed to be in the plan. No matter the rage of battle, soldiers still get erections when the shells stop dropping. The contractor's trailer near our bunker seemed a promising place for a liaison. While unloading food from a pickup truck, I snuck a small tin of ham into the inside pocket of my jacket; the meat was an excuse to invite the young woman to the trailer. She agreed to drop by, and I spent the afternoon anticipating her visit.

Alas, that evening about 6:00 p.m., I was walking toward my bunker when shooting erupted. I ducked behind a church – Wounded Knee seemed to contain as many churches as residents – and stayed there till the initial fusillade subsided. Amidst sporadic gunfire, I broke to the bunker more than a hundred yards away. Directly in front of us, the APC suddenly opened up with its 30-caliber machine gun. Our bunker was well constructed, with a dirt wall in front and topped with sandbags. We lay flat on the ground, the bullets streaking over us at a distance of about four feet, the red tracers sparking the night air into a deadly brilliance. These were the same machine guns I had been trained to use to kill Viet Cong. *You same same Viet Cong.*

More than sixty bullets sprayed the trailer where I had planned my evening tryst. I shared the can of ham with my friend Bradley.

A couple of days after the massive show of U.S. firepower, a ceremony took place at the Wounded Knee gravesite, conducted by Frank Fools Crow. Although eighty years old, he excited the young Indians earlier by proclaiming that "if you don't know how to fight the white man, I'll saddle up my horse, paint my face, and show you." Not very realistic, but exciting, coming from an elder. Many other elders watching the siege on television thought that Fools Crow and we were crazier than hell. That sentiment was shared by a number of younger Indian people, progressives. Afterward, we would meet them in the bars, the liquor loosening our tongues, and when it came to talking about Wounded Knee, we would tell them they should put on dresses. We then ended up pounding the hell out of each other.

Fools Crow held the prayer ceremony, and we all went to the mass grave and prayed for the dead, for the living, for survival, and for the unborn. Much to our surprise, it was then announced by the feds that the roadblocks were coming down, permitting free passage in and out of Wounded Knee. We were fools. We should have known you couldn't take white people at their word; they have proven that truism since 1492.

Someone carrying a money order for forty dollars proposed that a few of us go to town and get some essentials. It seemed like a good idea. Jimmy Irving, an older, Flathead man, drove the car, a 1962 four-door Chevy owned by my hippie-fighting partner, Sherman Jenkins. In front rode the sister of the Sisseton woman and Bradley LaPlant. The woman from Sisseton, a Blackfeet-Crow man named Jackson Red Horn, and I sat in the back. Jackson was a great bulk of a man, well over two hundred pounds; through the intricacies of Blackfeet blood and marriage, we were cousins; my blood mother was somehow related to the Shortfaces who were also his relatives.

We began our journey away from the madhouse of Wounded Knee, planning on returning as soon as we got some cigarettes and maybe something decent to eat. Speeding past the fallen roadblocks, we arrived in the village of Pine Ridge at about seven in the evening. Not finding any place open to cash a money order, we headed for Rushville, about twenty miles south in Nebraska. Rushville was one of those small farming towns that have their redneck racist corollaries in any part of the country – they'll take your Indian money, but don't try to date their daughters or drink in their Elks Clubs.[3] After cashing the money order and buying cigarettes and food in Rushville, someone announced it time to celebrate since the roadblocks were down and it presumably appeared that the siege of Wounded Knee was over.

We end up drinking a case of beer and a Texas fifth of vodka, more like a half-gallon. Merry we are, having just come through a siege. To me it's not much different than finishing up a day's work at the docks in Da Nang and then sneaking off to a bar and later a whorehouse before heading back to base. The Sisseton woman is pretty; she's been a powwow queen. The cigarettes, beer, vodka, and camaraderie are fine in the Nebraska night. The car was acting up, but it's something those of us who drive reservation cars know about. It backfires through the carburetor every now and then, no big thing; someone can set the timing when we get back. There's always a good Indian mechanic around, someone who grew up with these kinds of cars, who didn't have money to take these kinds of cars to the garage, and who can set the points using a matchbook.

We didn't return the way we came, because Jackson Red Horn claimed to know a shortcut. Nebraska, like all farm country states, unfortunately has numerous back roads that intersect and unless you really know your way around it's easy to lose your way. Soon we were lost and getting increasingly, laughingly drunk. Beer chased swigs of the vodka taken directly from the bottle. Indian drinking – no pretense of sociability, drinking for the effect. An Indian willing to give you the shirt off his back as you left Rushville with a bottle of whiskey at his disposal would be ready to take your head off by the time you got to Pine Ridge. That's how a lot of us drink.

Someone suggested we pull into a farmyard and ask directions. But this isn't Indian country.

We were hardly at a stop when the front porch light of the farmhouse flared and a farmer yelled, "What do you want?" We shout back that we were lost, and he wanted to know where we were going, and we shouted back Pine Ridge, and he sent us left and then right and stepped back into his house, and someone said we better get the hell out of there as he's probably loading his shotgun at the moment. After more zigs and zags through the farm country we came to what appeared to be a main road, which took us back to the road to Pine Ridge. So much for the shortcut.

The potatoes have done their work. A couple of times Jimmy Irving, copious in his attention to the vodka, drove in the ditch and someone suggested letting another person take the wheel. He wouldn't hear of it.

"Sherman loanded [his word] this car to me, and I'm responsible for it. He'd be pissed if somebody wrecked it."

So, there we were, stuck with a drunken chauffeur, who drink by drink was getting more belligerent. When Irving missed the road to Wounded Knee at Billy Mills Hall, I shouted at him to turn. He turned wide, and as luck would have it, a police van was approaching. We nearly hit the van head on, missing it by inches and veering at a crazy angle while our drunken driver tried to right us back on the path to Wounded Knee. Instantly, the police van turned around and soon was behind us, with its siren wailing and lights flashing. Irving asked us if we should try to outrun them, a fine quixotic question, but the car was ten years old, burned oil, and was belching through the carburetor. We advised him to stop.

The cops immediately put handcuffs on our chauffeur and put him in the van. Jackson Red Horn, having hit the vodka intensely, had already passed out and was slumped against the door behind the driver's seat. When the cops pulled the door open, he fell out headfirst onto the roadway; he came to already handcuffed. One of the cops stuck his head in the driver's side window and asked if anyone wasn't drinking. I spoke up and said I hadn't been drinking (a lie but I hadn't been drinking the vodka). He gave permission for me to drive the car home.

After about fifty yards, I shifted into second gear and immediately the car backfired through the carburetor and flames spurted out from under the hood. Damn the luck. Pulling over to the side of the road, we jumped out and popped the hood open. Fire was feeding off of gasoline that had come back through the carburetor and the old oil on the engine block. As soon as the hood opened, the increased air made the fire jump. Bradley and I attempted to throw gravel from the side of the road on the flames to douse them, but the gravel was scarce. Bradley suddenly remembered that we had stored some guns in the car – two pistols and ammunition were in the glove compartment. The fire was burning against the rear firewall, and it soon became clear that the heat might set the bullets off. I continued to uselessly throw gravel on the fire while telling Bradley to get the ammunition out and dispose of it.

On their way to the Pine Ridge jail, the cops apparently spotted flames high in the night sky in their rearview mirror. Bradley, thinking to help me douse the fire, gave the guns and ammunition to the sister who had been riding in the front seat. She was standing along the roadside holding the weaponry when Bradley spotted the cops coming back toward us. He shouted at the woman to get rid of the guns and ammo. She ran down the roadway about forty feet and tossed the guns and ammo onto the shoulder of the road and was racing back to the car when the police pulled up for the second time. They quickly put the fire out with a fire extinguisher. One cop then turned to the sister who had run into his headlights as he pulled up.

"Where did you come from?"

She replied that she had just gone down the road to take a pee.

He didn't believe her; I guess somebody returning from a pee at a flying run seems suspicious. Walking down the roadway with his flashlight, he discovered the discarded guns and ammo. We were all loaded into the van and were soon ensconced in the Pine Ridge jail.

The next day we were taken to Rapid City, where we were interrogated by FBI agents who asked us questions about ourselves and about Wounded Knee. We were given phone calls, and I managed to get hold of Jean. They wouldn't release us on bond at first because they feared we might return to Wounded Knee. We found out that the roadblocks had been reinstated just a few hours after they had been taken down; it had been a government ploy to decrease the population in Wounded Knee.

In our cell was Severt Young Bear, a traditional Lakota leader whose house we had stayed at upon our arrival in Porcupine.[4] A couple of white men also shared the cell with us, and we got along well with them. Not all white men and women are the same, of course; some have a different kind of a soul than those who end up running the government; some are not consumed by materialism, by greed, by the mainstream ideas of progress that are causing the sicknesses on the earth. There are a few who are willing to undergo the rigors of becoming outcasts and join with peoples of color in a quest for human rights. They had joined the occupation for their own reasons, mainly an interpretation of history different from the one they had been taught in their school systems.

I was confined to the Rapid City jail for ten days. My wife sent bond money after having some difficulty raising it. Bradley's family also raised his money, and we got out within hours of each other, as did Jackson Red Horn. We first went to a restaurant in Rapid City to eat. Red Horn, still bellicose, talked loudly and arrogantly about white people and their many sins against Natives while we ate. The white people sitting nearby pretended they didn't hear him. It made me feel uncomfortable, listening to Red Horn insult the other diners; they may have been decent enough people. But they were white, and Red Horn was angry and pushing the race card because he had just been in a white jail for effectively telling the U.S. government that what they had been doing for the past century was illegal, that the historical and legal processes that allowed white people to sit and eat in this particular restaurant were predicated upon the rape of people and land.

By this time the occupation was nearly a month old, and we considered going back to Wounded Knee. Having just spent time in jail, we were welcome at an AIM safe house in Rapid City. One of the organizers at the safe house said he thought the occupation was going to end soon and that what was next needed was a massive effort to educate people about what had really happened. He advised us to return to Montana, spread the truth, and help raise money for the AIM legal defense fund.

We went home. My daughter Dameon had been one day old when I had left for Wounded Knee, and I wanted to see her. As Vietnam veterans, Bradley and I could imagine the poor conditions in Wounded Knee – cold, with little food – and we weren't ready to rush back into the fray.

Once back on the University of Montana campus with my wife and family, I realized the spiritual ceremonies I had attended during my time among the Lakotas had opened something up, something vague and nebulous, but something important, something that had to do with defining the word Indian, what it really meant, from the Indian aerie.

And so I went home to the Blackfeet reservation. Being born Black-feet had led me in one direction; growing up in Cut Bank had altered that direction; Vietnam had veered me to the side of the trail considerably; and Wounded Knee had acted as a catalyst to launch me from one trail onto another far distant.

Epilogue

Such are the breakings of a tribal consciousness. I understand the U.S. government much better these days. I understand the Newtonian-Cartesian mind of the white man much better these days, and I remain a Viet Cong in his mind. He is not afraid of me; he is afraid of what he has done to me, and thus he is afraid of himself. As well he should be, because I have a long memory, and he should have thought of that when he came shooting and pillaging. Those thousands upon thousands of so-called illegal immigrants coming out of the south—Mexico, Central America, South America—are not illegal to me; they are my cousins; they are from this continent; they are my color; they are Natives. I am not as alone as the white man thought I was.

But we still have so much to learn. There is death and destruction nightly in the housing projects all across Indian Country in the twenty-first century. As I sit and write tonight on the campus of Sinte Gleska University in south-central South Dakota, I know that a half mile away, in the HUD housing project called Antelope, there are terrible things going on. Little kids are screaming, and as they cower in terror, their fathers thrash their mothers in drunken fits of violence. A mile or so beyond the Antelope housing project one finds the beginnings of comfortable farm homes occupied by white people; they sit serenely before television sets, unaware of or uncaring about what is happening a short distance from their homes, which sit on land that was taken by the gun and continues to be held by the gun and a culture of toughness.

Indians, those who try to live decently, without liquor or drugs or other pernicious influences in their lives, complain about the stereotype of the drunken Indian. But all stereotypes have some basis in fact. The fact is that through the years, from the time the Indian traders – Joe Kipp included – brought liquor among the Indians, we have really made fools of ourselves in the use of it. We've not only made fools of ourselves but have inflicted pain without measure in the use of alcohol.

Native American activists in the sixties and seventies recognized the necessity of sobriety. The cry for sober Native people became a mantra; it remains a mantra. The sobriety movement has been wide reaching and effective.

However, the statistics are grim when it comes to measuring the overall sobriety among young Indian people. The idealism of the activists of the sixties and seventies seems to have faded. Young Indian people can be seen and heard going down the reservation streets with subwoofers – or whatever those pieces of technology are called that make enough noise to seemingly raise the car right off the road – pounding rap music through the reservation hills. I listen. Once in a while the music coming from the cars will be powwow music, Red Bull, Young Grey Horse Society, or Black Lodge Singers. Or it will be country and western, white people singing in those mournful nasal cadences of lost love, lost wives, whiskey as a panacea for life's ills, music that a people trying to come out of a century of grief certainly don't need, but they go on listening to it. Sadness and depression have become so commonplace that the people growing up today don't know there was a time when reservation life wasn't like that. As I write this, we are getting ready to bury my oldest stepgrandson from an alcohol-related wreck. He was twenty-five. He is one of many thousands. We don't know what to do, don't know how to slow the carnage down.

Every reservation has a treatment center for alcoholics. The treatment centers spew out a lot of information: videos, books, pamphlets, conferences with powerful speakers. Traditional leaders – spiritual and secular – go into the schools and talk to the children, and still the carnage goes on. We weep and don't know what to do to save our children from this ubiquitous evil that has had a hard hand around our throats for more than a century.

There are those of us who have been down the road of liquor and finally, after many bad mornings of waking up with split lips, black eyes, and empty pockets, learned the hard lessons of drinking. Of course, our beatings and myriad hangovers notwithstanding, we could be said to be the lucky ones; the unlucky ones are dead, in prison, maimed, and in wheelchairs, and some lose their wives and children to liquor.

The Blackfeet have a prophecy. They predicted long ago that one day the plains would be on fire and the people who held to their spiritual ways would have to retreat to the mountains to survive. Other tribal people in the last generation have also foretold the fall of Western society. When schoolchildren are being gunned down left and right, when little girls are being pulled from their bedrooms and raped and kidnapped almost daily, I would hope that the Great Mystery would lower the boom on this insane machine- and money-crazed society. The people who believe that our grandmother earth is more than a metaphor, who believe the earth is alive, will survive.

This narrative will be seen by some simply as the highly subjective story of an Indian trying to get his bearings in the modern world. It's that. But at the same time I would ask the reader to look at its underlying and pervasive issues of race and dominance, issues that have shaped and formed this country since its earliest days. Nine-eleven centers very much on race and dominance; racial problems in America are not going away, at least not anytime soon. As I write this some blacks are clamoring for reparations for slavery, as well they should. They should be given land, though, not money – public land, forest service land, in effect, reservations for blacks. There is a lot of so-called public land in the American West. Blacks need some of that land so they can take their children there to learn about the natural world, to learn a respect that is a far different kind of respect than what can be learned from violence. I'm the Landlord of this country. I say give them some land.

The story in these pages reveals the first half of my life; the last half is a spiritual journey that began some thirty years ago with the smoking of the Sacred Pipe at the base of Mount Rushmore with a Lakota medicine man, Cielo Black Crow. At another time I will tell of those decades of spiritual growth, healing, empowerment through knowing the intimacies of ancient culture, and the sloughing off of tradition that is not useful today.

We often find ourselves and learn the twists and turns of the trail ahead by returning home, remembering, and learning. When I go home to the Blackfeet reservation, usually in the summer when I'm not teaching, I still drive to my folks' ranch on Cut Bank Creek. I often park on the high bluff that overlooks the ranch, the same bluff from which Meriwether Lewis looked out upon Cut Bank Creek in 1805. Nearly all the people who moved and lived in that particular place when I was a child are dead. The three houses our family lived in all burned to the ground. The first house burned when I was a toddler. It was a log house; a wood stove started the blaze. I burned the second house down in 1973 while drunk. A few years later, with Big John dead, his house burned down. It is a place of fire.

But something from my past, a past tested and refined by fire, endures and continues to grow. At the ranch, near the ashes of houses, stands a cottonwood tree. Big John, his wife, Bobby, and I planted that tree in 1962. Today it is a towering, flourishing cottonwood reaching high into the clear, cold Montana sky.

The Hopi prophecies say we are the people we have been waiting for. Maybe we are.

Notes

I. BRANDING

1. It is a bit confusing to people who are not from the Blackfoot Confederacy. People often ask what the proper designation is: Blackfeet or Blackfoot. According to the modern linguists who are compiling the native tongue into book and dictionary form, either designation can be used. So, Blackfoot or Blackfeet, no difference. Among the people of the Blackfoot Confederacy the word Blackfoot refers specifically to those people located east of the Canadian city of Calgary; their home, Siksika, means "black-footed person." In the present work I use Blackfeet and Blackfoot. I believe in the rhythms of poetry and sometimes one just sounds a little more euphonious than the other. I will refer to my people as the Pikuni Blackfeet, living in Montana; historically it was just Pikuni.

2. Blackfeet novelist and nonfiction writer James Welch has given quite a good account of the massacre in its fullness, in both his historical novel, *Fools Crow*, and his nonfiction book, *Killing Custer*.

3. My use of the racial term "white" has caused me grief. According to my Pikuni Blackfeet ID enrollment card, I'm seven-sixteenths Blackfeet and thus am actually more biologically white than Indian. I'm dark-skinned, however – the gods of genetics play strange tricks. I have cousins who have more Native blood than me but who are quite light. So, in using the term white I am referring not so much to skin color per se but rather to those pernicious attitudes that developed as Europeans moved west. There are some good

white people for whom the term is hardly applicable. The term as I use it refers to attitudes attendant upon the process of colonization and oppression.

2. LEARNING

1. When I came home on leave from the Marine Corps, Brian was in jail on the second floor of the Glacier County jail in Cut Bank. I talked to him through the bars. I still call his folks now and then, though I haven't talked to Brian in years.

2. Today, as an educator trying to convince young Indian students it is in their best interests to do their writing assignments, I can appreciate that slap from Leo Sherrod many years ago. It can be terribly frustrating to have students sit with blank looks when I ask them for their writing assignments and they offer lame excuses. I have never slapped a student, but my students are university students, not seventh graders. Still, there are some who are just as recalcitrant about turning in assignments as I was at the seventh grade level.

3. BECOMING

1. We didn't have much commerce with Sammons or any of the white farmers on the reservation. An occasional casual meeting on the streets of Cut Bank or out on the country roads was about the extent of our socializing with the white farmers.

2. When the reservations were broken into individual allotments, the government surveying teams drove iron pins into the ground, demarcating the boundaries of the allotment, with the allottees names printed on the pins lengthwise.

3. I deliberately chose July 13 as the date of induction because I wanted to participate in the annual North American Indian Days celebration on the Blackfeet Indian reservation. Though I watched the dancers for brief periods, the main attraction for young men like me was not the dance arena but the illicit booze. I spent most of the four days of the traditional celebration partying with other young men. Looking back, it is now patently obvious that though I

was raised by people who were only one generation removed from the buffalo hunters, they had, for all intents and purposes, been removed a far distance from the ceremonial life of their own people.

4. LEAVING

1. The ranch is deserted today except for a couple of buildings, but my Ford remains parked there, stripped but still sitting among the old farm machinery. A nephew of mine had bought a '57 Ford and pretty well cannibalized my Ford while I was in the Marine Corps. The fuel pump, generator, carburetor, water pump, and all the externals are gone. Still, there aren't too many men in their fifties who can say they still have the car they had as teenagers. It hasn't run since 1964, but I still own it. It sits at the base of a hill where it is believed Meriwether Lewis took his final northerly reading before turning south to rejoin Clark.

2. Like the renowned white psychic Edgar Cayce – I mention him because he also proved instrumental in my spiritual development – Spotted Eagle was unlettered as we understand education today. He knew things then that some quantum physicists are now discovering concerning how man relates to the forces of the universe.

5. FIGHTING

1. I had been a classmate of one of Louis's sisters in Cut Bank. His troubles stemmed from alcohol; he had broken into an officer's club for hard liquor. After my release from the brig I would not see him for another dozen years, not until he returned to Browning with a young white girlfriend who, it was rumored, had run away from home to travel with him. We visited a few times in Browning, and then he left for the city again. Several years later I heard he had died.

2. AIM has a national anthem; in the early years of the movement its members were the only voices I heard raised in that song. In later years, however, the AIM anthem would spread, and today it can be heard at major powwows. A song

only the revolutionaries were singing a generation ago is now mainstream. Years after I had stopped traveling with AIM, I was driving along a quiet country road on my way to hunt antelope on the Blackfeet reservation. It was the day after Thanksgiving. The radio was playing, and when the news came on, I heard the AIM national anthem coming over the airwaves. On Thanksgiving Day there had been a protest at Plymouth Rock, by Indians and white supporters, and they sang that song of unity.

3. Recently white men in Texas were sentenced for dragging a black man to death behind a pickup truck. Two weeks ago, as I write this, a black man went berserk and shot and killed several white men; a note found in his apartment alluded to racism as the reason for his murderous rampage. The more things change . . .

6. RETURNING

1. John Murray earned his PhD and went on to become an influential member of the Blackfoot tribe. His wife was president of the Blackfeet Community College. They retrieved one of the sacred Blackfoot medicine bundles from a museum through the Native American Graves Protection and Repatriation Act, a congressional act that allowed tribes to reclaim some of the sacred ceremonial items that were taken from them in the last century.

7. AWAKENING

1. Martin James Still Smoking is currently serving two consecutive life sentences on death row in the San Quentin prison for the murder of two women. A couple of times a year I write to him, and he answers. He is my adopted nephew. I have never disowned him.

2. Somebody in the remote past had it absolutely right when they labeled alcohol as *spirits*. People who drink see the label of a bottle of whiskey, distilled spirits, but they don't read it literally; it is literal, at least from a spiritual point of view. This point was made compelling once by an old man who was visiting the Blood reserve in Canada. Hailing from a Cree reserve farther north in

the province of Alberta, he had returned to the teachings of the Sacred Pipe after having gone through the travails of alcohol as a younger man. He was invited to speak at a conference devoted to rebuilding native communities, to restoring that sense of self that is essential to battling the downward pull of substance abuse, battling the inertia built over a century of white oppression. On the eve before his anti-alcohol lecture, taking place before a sweat lodge ceremony for the afflicted, he asked that a bottle of whiskey be brought to him. It was not wintertime so the lecture took place outside. The conference organizers were a bit hesitant to comply with his request. Was he going to get drunk at the last minute? Was he real? In the past century there have been many charlatans who have sprung up in Indian Country as Natives attempt to emulate the mores of white society, often ending up not emulating but parodying outsiders. He, however, was an acknowledged medicine man, so the organizers decided to follow his directive and brought him a full bottle of whiskey. When it came time to lecture the sodden Natives, he pulled the bottle of whiskey from under the lectern and held it so the label faced his audience. "See right here," he said, pointing to the label. "It says eighty-six proof." He let the idea of the number settle in and then told them that Indians have always had a belief in spirits – good and bad. "What that means, that number eighty-six, is that there are eighty-six spirits in this bottle, eighty-six bad spirits." With that, he poured the bottle of whiskey onto the ground. The lesson was doubly instructive; many of the men sitting in the audience had never thought about alcohol in a spiritual framework. They also knew that this old man was serious and truthful. Many had spent hours and hours panhandling on the streets to buy similar bottles of evil spirits, and here he was, pouring all that effort into the dust. Real serious. Big time.

10. JOINING

1. Much of the AIM leadership at that time was following a do-as-we-say-not-as-we-do philosophy, preaching against drinking while at the same time having a hard time staying away from the bars and drugs.

2. On New Year's Day, 2001, traveling back to the Winnebago reservation

where I was teaching at the tribal college, I stopped in Fort Robinson and went through the museum. Then I drove to the cow town where we had had the set to with the cowboys twenty-eight years ago. I went to the same bar, drank a non-alcoholic beer, and had a pleasant and humorous conversation with a cowboy wearing a big black hat. I didn't mention my previous appearance there. He must have been a small boy when that happened.

3. The blonde later told me she had never been in a fistfight in her life. This is not unusual for white women. Civilization dictates such. Indian women – at least those who grew up during the era when the reservation was filling with alcohol – fought. Fought over men. Fought over jealousy issues – clothing, cars, status, and jobs. I found it rather hard to believe the blonde when she told me she had never been in a fistfight in her life. Later I would talk to other white women who said they, too, had never been in a fight. I'm not sure what percentage of Indian women have been in pitched physical battles, but I assume the percentage is high. In the reservation bars it would be highly unusual to not see at least one fight. Very often the combatants were women. Once, I saw Indian women fighting with their upper clothes torn to shreds, and what a sight that was – not quite the same as topless dancing, but topless nonetheless. Topless by default. Topless by violence.

4. It would be twenty-one years before I would see the blonde again, in 1993 while working at the University of Montana. By that time she had been through a couple of marriages and had an eight-year-old daughter.

II. OCCUPYING

1. Other tribal leaders, such as longtime Blackfeet leader Earl Old Person – at that time the leader of the National Tribal Chairman's Association – were less helpful. Old Person had been elected to the Blackfeet Tribal Business Council in 1954. In the future he would be beaten twice, both times for two-year terms, in 1988 and 1998, yet he had returned to power by the twenty-first century. Many tribal councilmen and especially tribal chairmen don't even finish their two-year terms in office before they are unceremoniously dumped by the voters. The other eight members of the Blackfeet Tribal Business Council

come and go, including a few with college degrees, but Old Person hangs on. Out of a total of 47 years, Earl Old Person has been in office 43 of those years.

In the mid-seventies, at a ceremony on the Blackfeet reservation east of Heart Butte on White Tail Creek, Jim Little Dog, an oral historian of the Blackfeet, talked of Old Person's long political tenure. In the 1950s there was a little grouping of Cree people living just outside the agency town of Browning; the group of shanties was known locally as Cree Corner. In that ragged clutch of humanity, however, was a Cree metaphysician named Good Runner. He was crippled and was known as a healer and one who could see into the other world. Little Dog claimed that Old Person's father, Juniper Bull, took his son to the man of mystery for a ceremony; the old crippled man told them that Earl would never be beaten in an election. The story may be apocryphal, but the facts speak for themselves.

2. Once, in the middle of the night in Vietnam, I had actually suffered a rat attack while sleeping. The hardback tents we lived in had two-by-fours laid flat about four feet high for bracing; they ran the perimeter of the tent except for the door space. I awoke as in a nightmare as a rat jumped from the two-by-four onto my head. I felt its claws in my scalp. When I came to in an instant it leaped onto the floor, and I saw it scampering out the door. It didn't bite me.

12. RECLAIMING

1. One of the common stereotypes is that Indians smoke the peace pipe. We do that, but we also have war pipes. An Indian actor who has gained fame in recent years, Wes Studi, was interviewed a few years ago when TV violence was being discussed. He said something to the effect that he saw nothing wrong with the violence portrayed on TV, and that the world was a violent place. Of course he had a bit of a bias, as nearly all the roles Hollywood was offering him entailed his portrayal of a certain violence. But this is where Christianity has a place in the Indian world. The message of Christ's love, the message of peace, of non-violence, is essential in Indian Country right now; the violence of the old way was one of ordered violence, against enemies, against large violent

animals. Today the anarchic violence that pervades Indian Country is one born of the colonial process and is often a violence of self-hatred that is turned upon family members and members of one's own community, primarily through the use of liquor and drugs, agents which are not a part of our traditional cultures. Progressive Indians scorn those of us who wear our hair long, who Sundance, who vision quest, who attend sweat lodge ceremonies, who promote the re-learning of tribal languages, who understand at least a little of what Black Elk meant when he spoke of knowing "the power that is peace." In American society peace is not seen as a power. It is a condition that is tolerated. Americans are always waiting for the next war. And, again, I have to keep qualifying some of these statements, because I've been around white people for a half century and know how they think and react to some of the things being said here. There are some white Americans who truly work for peace. I am talking from a Native perspective and therefore speak primarily of the forces that govern the lives of my people and me, which, in this context, are the forces of the mainstream government that is traditionally dominated by white males and increasingly by white females. The rhetoric of today's political and economic leaders is no different than the rhetoric of those hippies in the wine shacks. I, myself, was a violent man at that time, but I was raised as an American. I was brainwashed and lived the brainwash to the hilt.

13. DEFENDING

1. When Timothy Leary's consciousness-seeking cohort, Ram Dass, went to India seeking higher knowledge, he did meditation and numerous esoteric practices for a long period of time, and one day his guru told him it was time to show his power. Ram Dass was giddy. He wondered what the guru would have him do to demonstrate the prowess he had gained during his training. When he reported to the guru to find out his task, the guru told him to go feed somebody. He was crestfallen. He thought maybe he would be asked to bend spoons with his mind or something similar. Instead, he was asked to go feed somebody. Do something holy. Feed somebody. The Indian people,

over there and over here, know something about man's evolvement – feed somebody.

2. Although Bradley didn't attend that Yuwipi ceremony, it affected him later after I described what had taken place. My account, coupled with whatever else was running through his mind, would drive him to the world of spirit-seeking a few years later when he returned from California, where he had been attending college. He would befriend an old man, Joe Eagle Child, who knew probably as much as anybody alive about the old-time songs and ceremonies. Eagle Child would live until the year 2000; he was ninety-five years old when he passed into the spirit world.

3. Rushville may be a bit more tolerant of Indians today, but not much. There are just too many drunken Indians out there, committing all manner of atrocities – against the whites, against each other – for white attitudes to change very rapidly.

4. In later years I would hear more about Severt as he continued to work among his people. Someone eventually wrote a book about him, and he died about the same time.

Index

Sweet Pine Hills, 3

Thu Ba, 40–41
Tombs, 54
Trail of Broken Treaties, 95–106
Triangle Bar z brand, 3

University of Montana, 82–86, 95, 109–
    10, 113–14
uss *General Mitchell*, 32
uss *Navarro*, 33

Valier MT, 80–81
Van Ness, Roger, 4, 13
Vietnam, 33–48; alcohol in, 36; arrival
    in, 33–34; awareness of, 27, 31; racism
    in, 43–47; rat attack in, 149n2
violence, 149ch12n1
Volunteers in Service to America
    (VISTA), 88–89

Wagner, Curly Bear, 87–89, 93
Warrior, Clyde, 88
Washington DC, 99–105
Waukazoo, Muriel, 121
Weaver, Don, 18
Welch, James (author of *Fools Crow*,
    Killing Custer), 143n2
Whiteman, Henrietta, 95–96
white people, 143n3
Wine Shacks of Missoula, 51, 110–13
Wounded Knee: defense of, 128–37;
    Kaw–liga at occupation, 109; reflec-
    tions on, 29; siege of, 114–15, 121;
    walk into, 125–27

Yellow Owl, John Joseph, 77–78
Yellowtail, T. R., 88, 89–92
Yokohama, Japan, 33
Young Bear, Severt, 121, 135, 151n4
Yuwipi ceremony, 122–24, 150n2

In the American Indian Lives series

I Stand in the Center of the Good
Interviews with Contemporary Native American Artists
Edited by Lawrence Abbott

Authentic Alaska
Voices of Its Native Writers
Edited by Susan B. Andrews and John Creed

Dreaming the Dawn
Conversations with Native Artists and Activists
By E. K. Caldwell
Introduction by Elizabeth Woody

Chief
The Life History of Eugene Delorme, Imprisoned Santee Sioux
Edited by Inéz Cardozo-Freeman

Chevato
The Story of the Apache Warrior Who Captured Herman Lehmann
By William Chebahtah and Nancy McGown Minor

Winged Words
American Indian Writers Speak
Edited by Laura Coltelli

Life, Letters and Speeches
By George Copway (Kahgegagahbowh)
Edited by A. LaVonne Brown Ruoff and Donald B. Smith

Life Lived Like a Story
Life Stories of Three Yukon Native Elders
By Julie Cruikshank in collaboration with Angela Sidney,
Kitty Smith, and Annie Ned

Mourning Dove
A Salishan Autobiography
Edited by Jay Miller

I'll Go and Do More
Annie Dodge Wauneka, Navajo Leader and Activist
By Carolyn Niethammer

Elias Cornelius Boudinot
A Life on the Cherokee Border
By James W. Parins

John Rollin Ridge
His Life and Works
By James W. Parins

Singing an Indian Song
A Biography of D'Arcy McNickle
By Dorothy R. Parker

Crashing Thunder
The Autobiography of an American Indian
Edited by Paul Radin

Turtle Lung Woman's Granddaughter
By Delphine Red Shirt and Lone Woman

Telling a Good One
The Process of a Native American Collaborative Biography
By Theodore Rios and Kathleen Mullen Sands

William W. Warren
The Life, Letters, and Times of an Ojibwe Leader
By Theresa M. Schenck

Sacred Feathers
The Reverend Peter Jones (Kahkewaquonaby) and the Mississauga Indians
By Donald B. Smith

Grandmother's Grandchild
My Crow Indian Life
By Alma Hogan Snell
Edited by Becky Matthews
Foreword by Peter Nabokov

No One Ever Asked Me
The World War II Memoirs of an Omaha Indian Soldier
By Hollis D. Stabler
Edited by Victoria Smith

Blue Jacket
Warrior of the Shawnees
By John Sugden

I Tell You Now
Autobiographical Essays by Native American Writers
Edited by Brian Swann and Arnold Krupat

Postindian Conversations
By Gerald Vizenor and A. Robert Lee

Chainbreaker
The Revolutionary War Memoirs of Governor Blacksnake
As told to Benjamin Williams
Edited by Thomas S. Abler

Standing in the Light
A Lakota Way of Seeing
By Severt Young Bear and R. D. Theisz

Sarah Winnemucca
By Sally Zanjani